Falconry

Falconry

A GUIDE TO TRAINING BIRDS OF PREY

SARAH-JANE MANARIN & KATE HARRIS

First published in 2025

Copyright © 2025 Amber Books Ltd

All rights reserved. No part of this publication may be reproduced,
stored in a retrieval system, or transmitted in any form or by any
means, electronic, mechanical, photocopying, recording, or otherwise,
without prior written permission of the copyright holder.

Published by
Amber Books Ltd
United House
North Road
London N7 9DP
United Kingdom
www.amberbooks.co.uk
Instagram: amberbooksltd
Facebook: amberbooks
Pinterest: amberbooksltd

Editor: Michael Spilling
Designer: Mark Batley
Picture researcher: Adam Gnych

ISBN: 978-1-83886-479-8

Printed in China

DISCLAIMER
This book is for information purposes only and the reader should
undertake any practices described in these pages at their own risk.
The techniques described in this book are dangerous and should
be approached with the utmost caution and following the correct
safety procedures. Neither the author or the publisher can accept
responsibility for any loss, injury or damage caused as a result
of using the blacksmithing techniques described in this book,
nor for any prosecutions or proceedings brought or instigated
against any persons that may result from using these techniques.

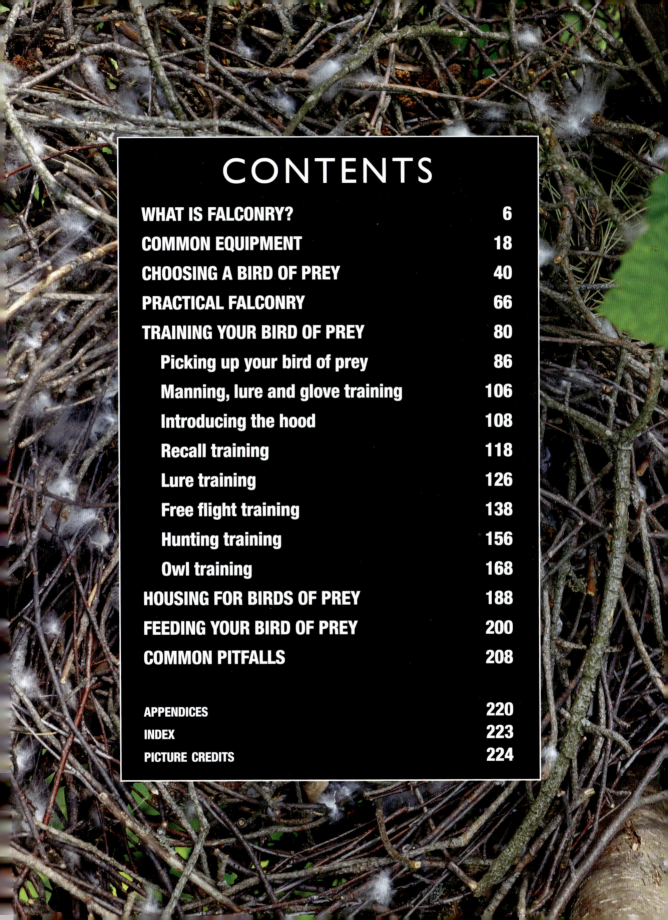

CONTENTS

WHAT IS FALCONRY?	6
COMMON EQUIPMENT	18
CHOOSING A BIRD OF PREY	40
PRACTICAL FALCONRY	66
TRAINING YOUR BIRD OF PREY	80
Picking up your bird of prey	86
Manning, lure and glove training	106
Introducing the hood	108
Recall training	118
Lure training	126
Free flight training	138
Hunting training	156
Owl training	168
HOUSING FOR BIRDS OF PREY	188
FEEDING YOUR BIRD OF PREY	200
COMMON PITFALLS	208
APPENDICES	220
INDEX	223
PICTURE CREDITS	224

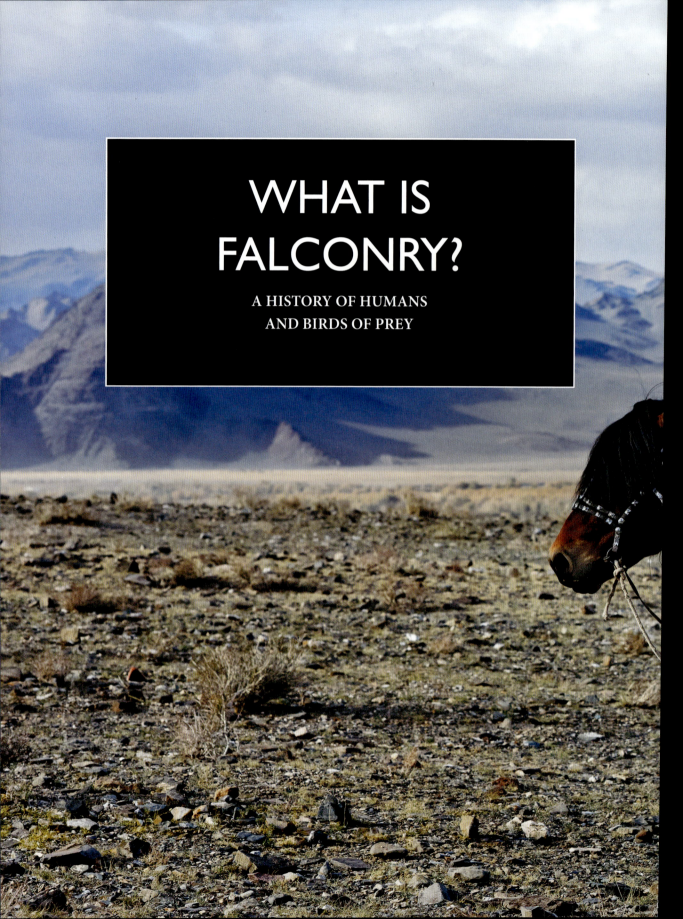

WHAT IS FALCONRY?

A HISTORY OF HUMANS AND BIRDS OF PREY

WHAT IS FALCONRY?

THE BOND BETWEEN BIRDS OF PREY AND HUMANS is a fascinating relationship and one that has existed for many thousands of years. Training a bird of prey is still integral within a variety of cultures in many countries. From training a particular species of raptor to hunt food for their families, to indulging in the entertainment of racing falcons as part of huge sporting events, falconry takes many forms and is once again gaining popularity, making it a captivating global hobby that is open to anyone with an interest in birds of prey. A person who hunted with falcons would historically be called a 'falconer',

Above: A PETROGLYPH FROM TEYMAREH, IRAN
Depictions of birds used in hunting could date the sport back as far as 7000 BCE.

Opposite: SCENE FROM THE ROOM OF THE LITTLE HUNT, VILLA ARMERINA, SICILY (FOURTH CENTURY AD)
Two men are looking for birds. One with bird in hand, the other with bird on shoulder, it is often thought these men represent falconers. They're depicted also carrying lime sticks, known as birdlime, which were sticks covered in an adhesive substance that were used at the time to trap birds.

and a person who hunted with hawks, eagles and buzzards an 'austringer'.

It's hard to trace falconry's ancient origins. However, the earliest written records contain such well-organized, technical details that it must certainly have been practised before the creation of writing itself. Indeed, petroglyphs found in the Teymareh region of northern Iran suggest employing birds of prey as a hunting partnership could date back as far as 7000 BCE.

Power and politics
Falconry was linked to politics and power in China, with written records dating back as far as the seventh century BCE. The writings describe techniques that are still used today. In fact, the imperial family in the Chu kingdom were using falcons, eagles and hawks in exactly the same way as we do today, which would potentially place the origins of modern falconry in China over 3,000 years ago.

In the fourth century BCE, in *Historia animalium*, Aristotle described falconry as a partnership between hunter and bird: 'Men hunt for little birds in the marshes with the aid of hawks. The men with sticks in their hands go beating at the reeds and brushwood to frighten the birds out, and the hawks show themselves overhead and frighten them down. The men then strike them with their sticks and capture them. They give a portion of their

WHAT IS FALCONRY?

Left: SEGMENT FROM THE BAYEUX TAPESTRY
The tapestry depicts the events leading up to the Norman conquest of England in 1066. One popular thought is that, as the depicted birds' wings don't reach the end of the tail, these birds are shortwings – i.e. hawks.

Opposite: PRINCE WITH FALCON
It is thought that this seventeenth-century watercolour shows Salim (the future Emperor Jahangir) wearing what appears to be Robes of Honor (*khil'at*) – detailed coats worn when riding or hunting. Here he appears to be calming his falcon.

Below: MAHARAJA SURAJ MAL WITH A HAWK
This eighteenth-century watercolour captures Maharaja Suraj Mal of Nurpur (r. 1613–18) posing with his hunting bird. The martial culture of Hindu courts celebrated the strength, speed and agility of birds of prey, and it was not unusual for rulers to depict their favourite animals.

booty to the hawks…' (book VIII, part 36). It's likely that the Greeks learned these techniques from the Persians.

Falconry was probably brought to Britain by European invaders. Hawks are referenced in both literature and art, including in the Anglo-Saxon poem the 'Battle of Maldon', and depicted on the Bayeux Tapestry, where we can see both William the Conqueror and King Harold holding birds of prey.

In Britain, birds of prey were a status symbol. Royal falconers were greatly revered. The 'Penhebogydd' (chief falconer) was fourth in command to the Welsh king and would enjoy advantages that denoted his status, such as the prince holding his horse or securing his stirrups when he was out hunting.

Royal protection
So important were they, birds of prey were vehemently protected by the Crown. Destroying an egg could lead to a prison sentence; taking a bird from the wild was punished by blinding the thief; and if someone was found to possess a bird deemed above their status, this was a crime punishable by cutting off the hand. Death was the ultimate punishment if one were to steal a trained bird in the fourteenth century.

Laws of ownership were laid out in the seventeenth century stating which birds one was allowed:

WHAT IS FALCONRY?

11

WHAT IS FALCONRY?

King: Gyrfalcon, either male or female
Prince: Peregrine falcon
Duke: Rock falcon
Earl: Tieral peregrine
Baron: Bastarde hawk
Knight: Saker
Squire: Lanner
Lady: Female merlin
Yeoman: Goshawk or hobby
Priest: Female sparrow hawk
Holy water clerk: Male sparrow hawk
Knaves, servants, children: Kestrel

Right: FALCONER OF KING JOHN II CASIMIR
This 1664 painting by Daniel Schultz the Younger shows Agha Dedesh alongside his sons and servants, his dog and a goshawk. The eldest son, styled Royal Falconer, was awarded this title by King John II Casimir (1609–72), King of Poland.

Below: JAMES VI AND I, KING OF SCOTLAND AND ENGLAND
The young King James VI (1566–1625) holding a sparrowhawk in what appears to be safety position.

FALCON SOUQ, QATAR
The Falcon Souq in Doha provides visitors with an insight into falconry, the heart of Qatar's traditions and culture.

They were not only signs of status; birds of prey were important enough to ostensibly use as currency. In the thirteenth century, the king of Norway sent eight grey and three white gyrfalcons to Edward I as a token of peace, and in the fourteenth century, Philip the Bold, Duke of Burgundy, offered 200,000 gold ducats (around £23.67 million today) for the return of his son, who had been captured by Sultan Bayezid of the Ottoman Empire. Bayezid turned down the offer, requesting in its place 12 white gyrfalcons.

Traditional sport
Falconry has travelled the world, leaving a rich and engaging trail in its wake. Over 3,000 years of history in the making, this traditional sport has been allowed to grow and develop, taking birds of prey from being tools to treasure. Today's falconers see these birds as much more: they are our hunting companions.

By definition, falconry is the training of a bird of prey so that it will return to the falconer's gloved hand once released to fly and/or hunt. Modern falconry tends to use a variety of raptors including falcons, hawks, buzzards and eagles to catch quarry (prey). A lot of people also keep owls in captivity to free fly, mainly as companion birds; however, the larger species of eagle owls can sometimes be used to hunt for prey, too.

In the UK, there is a strict season between 12 August and 1 February in which specific quarry can be caught with birds of prey, ensuring that no young wildlife is

Above: FALCONRY MARKET IN SOUQ WAQIF
So ingrained in Qatari culture is falconry, Souq Waqif possesses not only a prominent falconry market, but also a dedicated falcon hospital.

Opposite: POPULAR CULTURE
Film franchises like Harry Potter made owls incredibly popular and unfortunately, many people bought them as pets without knowing how to look after them. All birds of prey, including owls, require specialist care and training in order to give them a contented life. Here, a handler at a Harry Potter event is mishandling a barn owl – the bird should always be facing to the front of the glove so that the handler has proper control of the bird's feet and can assist the owl back onto the glove if it bates.

taken, and that the different species permitted to be taken are able to raise their young in good time, so that they may grow fit enough to outwit, outrun or outfly a raptor, if need be.

In modern society, it can be unusual to regard a relationship between a human trainer and a bird of prey: birds in captivity can be viewed through a negative lens. The beautiful thing about falconry is that you actually let the birds choose if they would like to come back to you. It is one of the most intense and successful bonds a human being can have with another living creature: a symbiosis between two separate species, which involves trust, reward, training and dedication.

Through various training techniques that we will explore further in this book, the foundations of falconry lie within the bond you build, which is rooted in the bird's natural survival instincts and its feeling safe in your care. By allowing your bird of prey to fly free and act out all of their natural desires and instincts on a daily basis, you are helping to ensure that the bird will want to return to you for food, companionship and shelter.

COMMON EQUIPMENT

THE TOOLS FOR MANAGING YOUR BIRD

COMMON EQUIPMENT

To keep your bird of prey safe throughout their lifetime with you, there are essential pieces of equipment that must be used as part of their training and ongoing maintenance.

A bird of prey that is being kept for falconry will have some form of permanent equipment placed on their legs. This equipment is called 'furniture' and is one of the most important parts of falconry because it allows the falconer to handle the bird without the worry of being injured in the early stages of training, giving the falconer more control over when to release their bird out in the field – there could be danger up ahead that the bird is unaware of, so it is essential that the bird can be safely held on the glove and flown free only when it is appropriate to do so. As a falconer, you can either make all of the furniture yourself or purchase the entire kit online from a reputable falconry supplier.

The following are the most common and fundamental pieces of equipment that are used in falconry today. Not much has changed from the initial furniture and methods that were used thousands of years ago; however, we are blessed with the existence of digital scales and GPS telemetry now, which does make life a lot easier!

Weighing scales

There are a variety of scales that are suitable for falconry – we use electronic, digital scales to weigh all of our birds and they are extremely accurate for small and large birds of prey. Most digital scales will have to be modified to make them suitable for falconry, however; you will need to attach a perch on to the base of the scales so that your bird can sit comfortably and steady while you take their weight. With digital scales, you must check the batteries regularly because they can be less accurate when they are losing power, so if a weight seems a bit strange, it may be time to put a fresh lot of batteries in.

The other alternative is to buy a set of balance scales where you perch the bird on one end and then apply different weights on the other until the scales balance and you can take the weight of the bird from there. These are slightly less accurate due to the restrictions on weights available so it can be slightly tricky to weigh very small raptors on these types of scales.

Either option is perfectly fine and the most important thing is that you can register the weight of your bird however you feel most comfortable. Remember, the scales are one of the most important parts of falconry for weight management and health, so get a good, sturdy set and they will last you for many years.

Block and bow perches

When you are tethering your bird of prey during the initial training process, you will need a block or bow perch. These are either weighted so that you can stand

Left: WEIGHING
A falcon being weighed on traditional weighted scales. The bird is placed on a modified perch at one of end of the scales and weights are put on the other side of the scales until the beam is balanced.

Opposite: T PERCH & WEIGHING SCALES
A Eurasian eagle owl sits on scales using a T perch.

COMMON EQUIPMENT

COMMON EQUIPMENT

them on hard ground or they will have spikes at the base of the perch so that you can press them into grass or soft ground. Depending on the design of your aviary, you can choose the most suitable option for your particular environment.

Block perches have a flat top for the bird to sit on and are usually preferred for falcons and eagles, which will naturally sit on flat surfaces such as cliffs and rocks in the wild, so it is more comfortable for their feet. They usually have artificial grass on the top of the perch, which is what the bird will actually sit on. This helps prevent bumblefoot and pressure sores in the bird's feet. They have a moveable ring at the bottom of the perch where you can tether your bird safely.

Opposite & below: BOW PERCH
Harris's hawk on a bow perch. Bow perches can also be wrapped in rope instead of astroturf and rubber (pictured below).

COMMON EQUIPMENT

Bow perches are usually favoured for any species of bird that prefers to sit on branches in the wild: their feet will grip on to the round, rubber top with ease. The rubber material is usually grooved or it will have lots of raised bumps running along the top of the perch – again, this is to prevent pressure sores and bumblefoot in the bird by spreading the weight across different parts of the foot.

They have a moveable ring at the side of the perch that should reach all the way over the top and to the other side of the perch so that you can tether your bird safely without it getting tangled by the leash.

Left: HOOD
Hooded falcon at rest on a block perch.

Below: ANKLETS & FLYING JESSES
Falcon wearing anklets, flying jesses secured in safety position, on the falconer's glove.

24

Anklets

A fundamental part of falconry furniture is the anklets. These are effectively bracelets that are usually made of soft leather and have an eyelet fitted to create a hole in the leather that the jesses can thread through. The anklets are wrapped round the bird's leg and are designed to stay on the legs permanently – they are replaced when the material is worn (usually on an annual basis).

Each anklet needs to be modified for the bird it is being fitted to; they are the bird equivalent of shoes – even the same species can have different-sized legs, and will therefore require different-sized anklets. For this reason, more experienced falconers tend to make

Left (all): ANKLETS
There are many different styles of anklets on the market today and all of them can be made by the falconer, too. They are made of leather and usually have an eyelet or some form of locking mechanism to hold the anklet on the bird's foot. Here are four examples:

Leather anklet with pin/rivet closing mechanism (top).

False aylmeri-style anklet, which is removable and wraps round the bird's leg to secure (upper middle).

Aylmeri-style anklet, which will be secured by the jesses on the bird's foot (lower middle).

Anklet with holes to secure to the bird's leg with an eyelet (bottom).

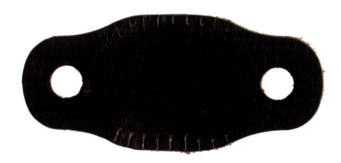

25

COMMON EQUIPMENT

All photographs: BRAIDED EQUIPMENT
As well as traditional leather equipment, there are now many types of braided falconry equipment, including:

Braided anklet, which fits like a false aylmeri (top).

Braided anklet showing the knot and loops that provide the wrapping mechanism that will fit it on to the bird's leg (middle left).

Braided flying jess attached to leather anklet (middle right).

Swivel (below left).

Braided leash (below right).

BALD EAGLE
A bald eagle being called into the falconer's glove, showing a wide variety of different falconry furniture.

COMMON EQUIPMENT

Above: ALL-IN-ONE
Traditional, all-in-one anklet and jess template made in leather. This design wraps round the bird's leg and is made from one piece of leather.

Right: LEASH

their own equipment, as opposed to buying a generic-sized anklet from a supplier; it works out cheaper in the long run to buy a large leather hide and make perfectly fitting equipment, bespoke for your birds.

The soft leather absorbs any shock from sudden movements and, like a collar left on a dog, the bird is perfectly happy to wear a pair of anklets its entire life.

Anklets should be changed once a year, to avoid them becoming brittle and breaking. Ideally, they should also be waxed regularly, so that the leather remains supple and comfortable for the bird.

There are many different styles, but all have the same purpose: to be the anchor for the jesses.

Mews jesses
A jess is a strap that goes through the eyelet on the anklet. They come in a variety of braided nylon versions, though they were traditionally made from leather. They are fed through the eyelets on the anklets to tether a bird of prey; they feature a slit at the end, so that they can be folded over a swivel.

The bird of prey needs a pair of jesses so that the falconer can safely control the feet and therefore talons of a bird when it is being trained, as well as to tether the bird for medical assistance.

Flying straps/flying jesses
These are identical to the mews jesses except for one major difference: they have no slits at the bottom of the leather.

The reason this flat piece of leather has no slits at the end is that when a bird is flying out in the field, a branch could snag through the slits of a pair of mews jesses, which could be disastrous for the bird. If they are hanging upside down by the branch, unable to free themselves from the mews jess, they may die if they are not retrieved quickly enough.

Flying jesses can either be placed on the anklets permanently, or removed each time the bird is flown – the type depends entirely on the preferences of the individual falconer.

Swivel
The swivel is a small piece of metal that can rotate, and is usually made of two parts.

The top part is a rough 'D' shape, which the mews jesses can be folded over, to hold them in place, when tethering a bird.

The second piece of the swivel is a rotating loop through which the leash is threaded; because this part of the swivel can rotate, it minimizes the risk of

COMMON EQUIPMENT

the leash becoming tangled. It is an amazing piece of equipment – low-tech, but so effective!

It is designed purely to aid the tricky job of securing two jesses with only one hand. As the jesses can be threaded through the middle of the D loop and then folded back on themselves, the falconer can easily secure a bird of prey after its flight with one hand, and then the leash can be put through the rotating loop, at the bottom of the swivel, to further secure the bird. The leash is then usually tied on to the glove, so the bird is safely attached to the falconer.

Leash

The leash for birds of prey is similar to leashes for other animals – they are long leads, used to control the bird in a safe area until it is ready to fly.

They are usually made of nylon, because it will not break or stretch like leather does.

Leashes vary in length and thickness. What type you choose depends on which species of bird you are trying to train, though all have the same job to do. They are threaded through the loop of the swivel and tied to whichever perch the bird will be sitting on during the training process.

Pouch/pot

Most falconers will have a falconry flying jacket that contains a food pouch or pot, where food is stored

Below: FLYING JESSES
Owl in flight wearing anklets and flying jesses.

COMMON EQUIPMENT

Left:
LEATHER HOOD

Middle: LEASH
Nylon leash showing swivel attached to one end and traditional falconry bells and leather anklet.

Bottom: LEATHER HOLE PUNCH TOOL

Opposite:
TELEMETRY TRACKER
A pocket link receiver (left) and transmitter (right).

A falcon fitted with a transmitter is shown in flight (far right).

COMMON EQUIPMENT

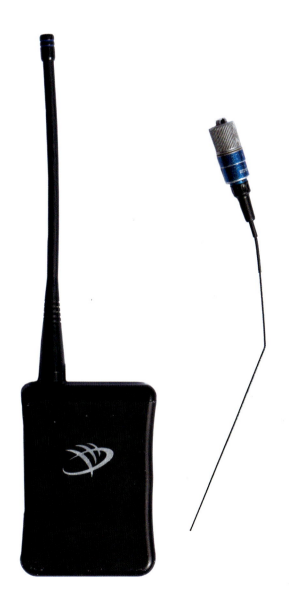

an idea of the direction and distance the bird has gone, if it flies out of sight.

GPS trackers make life a lot easier – you can download an app to your phone and the transmitter shows you exactly where your bird is.

A good telemetry system is invaluable, and everyone who flies birds of prey freely should always, without fail, attach a tracker to their bird.

Not doing so runs the risk of losing your bird, which is careless – and unacceptable in today's world. A non-native bird of prey living wild can cause unheard-of damage to the natural ecosystem, and this is totally avoidable.

Most importantly, there is a high chance that your bird of prey would not survive in the wild, so fast retrieval is the kindest thing to do for your feathered friend, and the telemetry allows you to do that quickly and efficiently.

during a bird of prey's flight. These should be cleaned after use and thoroughly disinfected to maintain good welfare and hygiene for the bird.

Telemetry tracker

Telemetry trackers comprise a transmitter and receiver and are without a doubt the most important piece of equipment to have fitted to your bird of prey when you are at the free flying stage of their training.

The transmitter is secured to the bird before its free flight – either by a tail mount or attachment to the anklet – and the receiver is able to pick up the signal from the transmitter. This allows the falconer to have

Gauntlet

This is the leather glove that falconers use to carry their birds around, and call to, during their flight. These can be single-, double- or triple-layered and you can even get leather extension 'sleeves' that cover almost your entire arm for handling large eagles. It is important to select the right thickness of glove for the particular species of bird that you wish to train – some birds have extremely powerful feet that can go right through a single-layered glove.

The gauntlet or glove is there to protect the falconer from any injuries that may occur from a bird's talons

COMMON EQUIPMENT

Above: GAUNTLET

Above right: FOOD POUCH

Right:
LEATHER LURE PAD
With rope and handle.

during the handling process, but it also allows the bird to sit comfortably and feed on the glove of the falconer. This creates a long-lasting bond as the bird will start to see the glove as a very comfortable dinner plate and will be looking to return to it as soon as possible!

Usually the gauntlet is on the falconer's least dominant hand, as they will need their good hand to tie and untie the 'falconer's knot'. There are, of course, left- and right-handed gauntlets to cater for this preference.

Lure

This is normally a leather pad, which is attached to the end of a piece of rope; the rope is wound around its handle, and the falconer can then swing the lure in one hand, while holding the rope's slack in the other.

Lures are used to engage falcons in flight. Some falconers now train several species of raptor to the lure because it can help with retrieval out in the field.

A swung lure is a very attractive target for a trained bird of prey, because it comes to know that there is a big reward attached to it. Food is tied around the leather pad and, when swung, it replicates a bird in flight – for raptors specializing in catching birds (falcons and some hawks), the lure is irresistible.

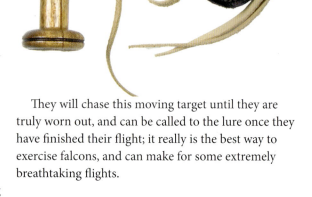

They will chase this moving target until they are truly worn out, and can be called to the lure once they have finished their flight; it really is the best way to exercise falcons, and can make for some extremely breathtaking flights.

Creance

The name 'creance' comes from the late fifteenth century from the French word *créance*, which means 'faith'. In falconry terms, it denotes a cord used to retain a bird, which is *peu de créance* ('of little faith'); a bird that cannot yet be relied on will have the creance fitted. The creance can be removed once the bird of prey has good recall over a long distance.

It is a long cord, which is usually coated with oils or wax to stop it snagging on foliage. Like the lure, it is wound around a handle so that the falconer can hold the creance and keep it secure, while the other end of the cord is tied to the swivel of the bird.

We only use a creance on birds that are in training, when we are trying to get an idea of their flying weight before we let them fly free. (Flying weights are explained later.)

Coping files

When a bird of prey has an overgrown beak, it needs to be filed into shape, to stop the bird developing complications when eating. This process is called 'coping'.

If a beak is left too long for a considerable amount of time, it can break or crack, which can be extremely painful for the bird; a lot of repair work would then be necessary to stop further pain and the risk of infection. Both the upper and lower mandible of the beak need filing, in captive birds of prey.

It is inexcusable to see birds of prey that cannot close their beaks because a falconer has not carried out coping regularly enough. Overgrown beaks

Above: STAYING SAFE
An Aplomado falcon wearing telemetry on its anklet.

occur in captive birds of prey because, unlike their wild counterparts, captive birds are fed high-quality, nutritional food daily, so their bodies are not starved of the essential vitamins and minerals needed for growth. This means their beaks grow rapidly; they are made of keratin (the same material as our hair and fingernails), so, just as when we eat well, our hair and nails grow longer and at a faster rate, so it is with a bird's beak.

The process of coping a beak is very simple and can be likened to having your fingernails filed into shape. It must be done carefully, though, holding the bird securely to avoid the risk of a nasty nip or grab from the bird, or damage to its beak.

TRAVEL BOX

To transport your bird of prey safely and, of course, to pick the bird up initially, you will need a falconry travel box that is the correct size for the species. A falconry travel box is a fully blacked-out box with air holes and a perch that runs through the middle so that the bird can sit calmly and comfortably throughout the journey.

COMMON EQUIPMENT

Left:
COPING FILE SET

Below:
CLAW CUTTERS
Falconer trims talons with a pair of claw cutters.

To cope your bird, you will need a set of coping files and a pair of animal claw cutters to safely trim the ends off the beak and talons. You can either do this yourself or any vet will assist you.

Donor feathers (imping)

Sometimes a bird can damage their feathers either within their aviary or when out flying free. We have had crows swoop in on our birds while they are flying and literally grab hold of their tail feathers to snap them and destabilize our bird on the wing, for example.

If a bird of prey damages their primary feathers in the wing or any of their tail feathers, it can make it harder for them to fly and steer. The process of 'imping' is when the falconer repairs the feathers by using a donor feather.

Donor feathers are normally moulted feathers from that bird from the year before, so it is very important that you keep the moulted feathers of your bird just in case you require them for imping.

The donor feather is glued to the shaft of the broken feather on the bird's body – this is usually done using a dowel and glue so that the donor feather can be securely fitted to the original feather shaft.

When the imping process has been done, the feather will be complete and fully functional again.

LICENSING AND THE LAWS SURROUNDING FALCONRY

In the UK, there is very little legislation, and anyone can legally obtain any species of raptor.

Native birds that have been bred in captivity require what is called an Article 10 certificate, which proves the bird was not taken from the wild – this relates to the bird's closed ring, which will have been put on one of the young bird's legs at around 10 to 12 days old.

A falconry licence is required by law in the UK for anyone flying a bird of prey free in a public area. However, this only indicates what the bird is allowed to hunt – it does not address the suitability and competency of the owner.

Birds of prey are extremely difficult to train and can easily be killed through poor weight management and lack of attention to their welfare needs. Anyone wanting to buy or adopt any bird of prey should volunteer at a falconry centre first or join a reputable falconry club where a mentor can be assigned to you. That way, you have all the support and training required by knowledgeable falconers to make sure that your bird will have a long, happy life with you.

In the US, a sponsor must be found to sign off the aspiring falconer as a falconer. Each state has different laws on falconry so anyone wishing to start their falconry training in the US is advised to contact their state wildlife department or agency to get the correct advice on how to proceed as well as a list of potential falconry clubs that can be contacted.

To find a suitable sponsor, a falconry apprentice in the US would typically meet other falconers via their state falconry club and receive a minimum of two years' training under a general or master-class falconer. A written exam is then required as part of the state federal regulations before your permit or licence will be granted to you, and you are then allowed to obtain your first bird.

Apprentice falconers work to obtain their Apprentice Falconers Licence and Trapping Permit then, working with their sponsor, they are only allowed to trap a red-tailed hawk or an American kestrel to train.

Falconry in the Middle East requires the falconer to obtain a hunting licence to fly the bird free at quarry. This only lasts for one season and the falconer must be a citizen of the country, at least 18 years old and have the falcon registered in the Falcon Registration System of the Ministry of Climate Change and Environment.

Very similar to the US, falconers in the Middle East will usually learn from a sponsor and have to trap their first bird using either nets or snares. Peregrine and saker falcons are usually the favoured birds of prey for falconry in the Middle East and they are trained to hunt the Houbara bustard and sand grouse.

A new law was passed in Abu Dhabi from October 2023 that prohibits falconers from taking any other wild quarry apart from the Houbara bustard, to help with conservation and biodiversity in popular hunting areas. Still a large part of Arabic heritage and culture, it is estimated that the UAE assigns over £21 million per year towards the protection and conservation of wild falcons. In fact, they have two dedicated, state-of-the-art falcon hospitals located in Abu Dhabi and Dubai. The Abu Dhabi Falcon Hospital, the largest dedicated falcon hospital in the world, was founded in 1999 and sees around 11,000 falcons per year.

TALON CLIPPING AND COPING

In captivity, birds of prey get a high-quality diet on a daily basis. This means that their beak and talons will grow at a much faster rate than those of a wild bird. It is up to the falconer to maintain good beak and foot health with the birds of prey in their care.

TALON CLIPPING: Your bird of prey might bate when approached on the glove so wait until the bird calms down before casting it ready for talon clipping and coping.

1. To help calm the bird while it is on the glove, the falconer can gently restrain the bird of prey by wrapping their hand over its wings from the back.

2. This allows another person to wrap the bird in a casting jacket (shown) or towel so that the bird can be restrained while being clipped.

TALON CLIPPING AND COPING

3. A casting jacket can be secured from the front with Velcro to hold the bird still while it is being handled.

4. When the bird is wrapped up in a casting jacket or towel and is restrained it can be lifted from the falconer's glove.

5. Hold the bird firmly at the shoulders to keep the wings restrained in the casting jacket or towel.

6. Always hold both feet securely during the coping process.

7. When the bird is secured by the body and feet, you can approach to trim the talons.

8. A falconer trimming a bird's talons with claw clippers.

TALON CLIPPING AND COPING

9. A Harris's hawk's talons after being trimmed.

COPING: In order to health check and cope your bird you will need to open its mouth gently. Place your thumb tip into the corner of the bird's mouth in order to hold the beak open.

1. A Harris's hawk having her top mandible filed down with a metal coping file.

TALON CLIPPING AND COPING

2. A Harris's hawk having her bottom mandible filed down with a metal coping file.

3. Close the beak to see if any more material needs to be filed away. Both mandibles should close easily on a nicely shaped beak.

4. The bird should be able to open and close their beak easily. Keep a slight hook on the end to help it tear up food when eating.

5. Moisturizing cream ready to be applied to a bird's foot as part of healthcare maintenance.

6. Evenly spread the moisturizing cream on your hand before applying it to the bird's foot.

7. Rub the moisturizing cream into the bird's skin until there is no excess residue on any of the foot.

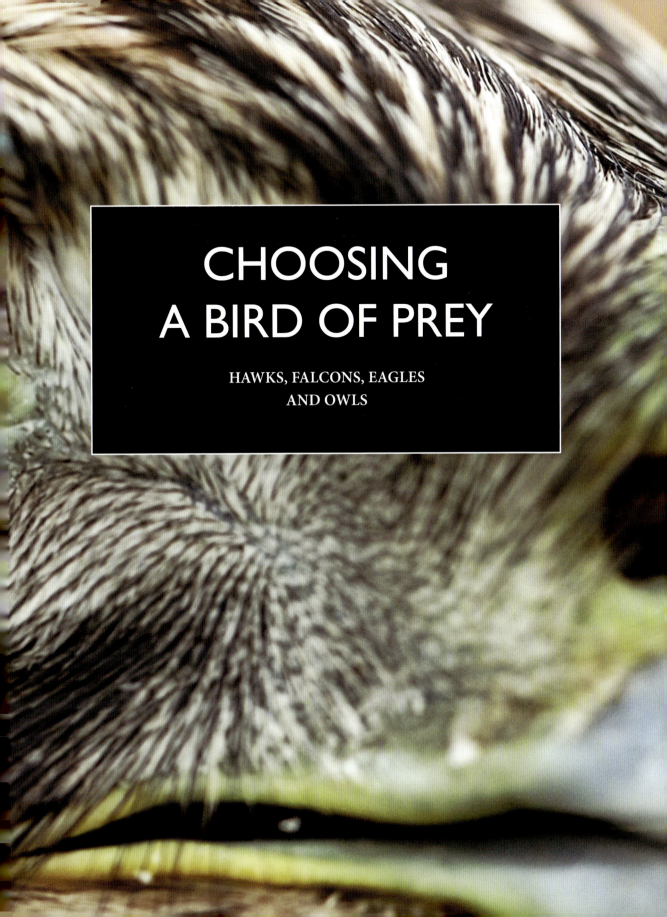

CHOOSING A BIRD OF PREY

HAWKS, FALCONS, EAGLES AND OWLS

CHOOSING A BIRD OF PREY

THE SPECIES OF BIRD that a falconer chooses to train will depend entirely on their experience, room to house the bird and what they would like to fly the bird for: Would you like a bird to hunt quarry with each year and then rest the bird in the summer so that it can moult out? Are you interested in flying a particular species of bird free in a private area or a piece of land you have permission to fly on? Do you just want a companion bird that will fly free to your glove without the need to hunt anything? These are the initial questions that must be asked by any sensible falconer looking for their first bird.

When considering taking on a bird of prey, it is important to understand the commitment required – not only in the bird's initial training, but every single day of its life. Most raptors in captivity live very long lives: 25–40 years is not unheard of, depending on the species, and unless you have a knowledgeable person who can help to feed and fly your bird in your absence, you must be present each day – so no more holidays for you.

Your bird will rely on you for companionship, food and entertainment. Imagine how awful it would be for your bird to just sit on its own all day without any attention or chance to fly. You are entirely responsible for the bird of prey you bring into your life, and this decision should not be taken lightly.

It is always the best advice to say: do not get a bird of prey unless you have the time, dedication, land to fly the bird and money not only for the initial set-up and equipment, but for vet fees and any maintenance on the bird and its housing in the future. Instead, volunteer at a falconry centre or go to a falconry club meet so that you can be around and work with the birds but without the commitment requirements.

People who are serious about falconry and owning their own bird would by this point have worked or volunteered at a bird of prey centre or zoo to gain as much practical advice on how to look after and train a raptor, obtained a falconry licence if they are planning to fly their bird of prey on public land, built their aviary and got all of the relevant equipment and falconry furniture for their chosen bird, and be working with a mentor who can help them with the training of their bird.

So, what birds of prey are available for falconry? Listed below are the most common.

Red-tailed hawk (*Buteo jamaicensis*)
Originating in North America, the red-tailed hawk is a large species of buzzard. They are heavily built and have a wingspan of about 90 to 135cm (3–4.5ft). They are found throughout North America, as far north as Alaska, and also have populations in the West Indies. This species is extremely common throughout the west of North America and they are well-known for being strong, confident hunters of varying types of prey, including small mammals, rodents, crabs, lizards, birds and invertebrates.

Because red-tailed hawks are far from fussy when it comes to what they eat, they have become an extremely common bird for use in falconry as, when the bird is trained, it flies and hunts over most types of terrain and can take larger prey species such as hares and squirrels, which other birds of prey would struggle to catch and hold on to. In the US, an apprentice falconer is able to catch and train the red-tailed hawk as their first bird, so it is seen by many as a very good bird to begin their falconry career with.

The red-tailed hawk varies in size depending on the sex of the bird: males can weigh between 737g and 1.1kg (1lb 10oz–2lb 8oz), whereas the females tend to be much larger and can weigh between 1.2kg and 1.5kg (2lb 10oz–3lb 5oz). Males can catch and hold anything up to the size of a large rabbit, whereas females have been known to catch and hold hares and foxes, so which sex would be best for a falconer depends entirely on what the falconer wishes to hunt. Because this is a larger species, there is far less risk of an inexperienced falconer causing harm to the bird when they are handling it and there is a larger margin of error when it comes to weight control.

Red-tailed hawks can be trained to fly from the falconer's fist directly at its quarry, or they can be trained to soar overhead, waiting for the falconer to flush out prey, and then perform an incredible, powerful stoop to build up speed and ambush the prey from a greater height.

They are very beautiful birds. In their first year, the red-tailed hawk is a lovely, detailed patchwork

Opposite: BUZZARD SPECIES
The red-tailed hawk, *Buteo jamaicensis*, is a North American species of buzzard.

43

of cream, dark brown on the back and tail, and a beautiful, mottled, light brown colouration running down the underside of their body. The red tail does not come through until after their first moult when the bird reaches adulthood.

Over time, they develop more ginger hues throughout their body, and the eyes turn from a light silver to a dark brown colour. There are many different colour variations in the plumage of the red-tailed hawk and this depends on where they are found throughout their range. Some red-tailed hawks appear to be almost black whereas at the other end of the scale are very light-coloured individuals; the tail remains red in all colour variations.

While the red-tailed hawk is extremely popular in America, it has never been quite as popular in Europe because it is more stubborn to train than the extremely popular Harris's hawk, and goshawks are traditionally the preferred choice of bird to fly at game in these areas.

Red-tails can be very temperamental during the training process; they have extremely powerful feet and can cause serious injury to an inexperienced handler. They also have a naturally aggressive personality and a very independent nature, so care is needed in the initial training stages to build a strong relationship and bond with the bird to get a good flying partner.

When a red-tailed hawk has been fully manned (tamed) and trained, they are a great all-round hunting bird that will catch a variety of prey for you. They need consistent training throughout their life so that they do not revert back to a wilder nature, but they are very forgiving and intelligent birds that will make a fantastic first raptor if you have the right mentor.

Due to the variety of different quarry you can take and the exciting flying styles that they can perform, a red-tail is a fantastic choice for any falconer who wants a bird to fly for fun and success out in the field without the need for any other species.

Harris's hawk (*Parabuteo unicinctus*)
One of the most popular birds used in falconry today is the Harris's hawk. This is a large species of hawk that originated in South America – they are widespread

Below: HUNTER IN FLIGHT
Red-tailed hawks will hunt anything from small rodents through to foxes.

AMERICAN NATIVE
Native to the southwestern US, the Harris's hawk can be found as far south as Brazil. They are hardy birds that are very popular in falconry due to their cooperative nature.

HAWK IN FLIGHT
Harris's hawks are naturally social, something that can be useful for falconers with more than one species.

throughout Chile, Argentina and Brazil, where they are locally common. Interestingly, they are not a true hawk, as their name suggests. Rather, they are a type of buzzard, as reflected in their Latin name, *Parabuteo*, which means 'buzzard-like'. They are very attractive birds – adults are dark brown throughout the body with rusty red legs/wing patches and a very striking white band on the end of their tails. Juveniles have similar colouration to the adults but have light streaks on the body and a zebra-coloured stripe pattern on their tail.

Harris's hawks vary greatly in size – males are smaller than females, which is typical of most raptors. However, even within the same sex there can be huge differences in the weight and wingspan of individuals. Typically, a male Harris's hawk will weigh between 510g and 595g (1lb 2oz–1lb 5oz) and the females can weigh between 907g and 1.4kg (2–3lb). The wingspan of a Harris's hawk is usually between 90cm and 120cm (3–4ft). Harris's hawks are strong, stocky birds with long legs and very large, powerful feet, which they use to catch a huge variety of prey.

In the wild, Harris's hawks have an amazing superpower that is extremely rare in the bird of prey world: they are sociable birds and will live in cooperative groups with other individuals of the same species. These groups are called a 'cast' and can consist of three to seven birds. Living within a pack makes them highly successful at hunting as they work together to flush out prey and tackle it on the ground. They can also alert each other to potential dangers and will scream when they feel threatened – when the scream is heard by the other cast members, they can either work together to drive the threat away or get as far away as they can from the potential problem as quickly as possible.

Harris's hawks will try and catch absolutely anything: jackrabbits, hares, snakes, lizards, squirrels, small- to medium-sized birds, rodents and even carrion if there is nothing else available.

For falconry, you simply cannot get a better bird than a Harris's hawk. Whether you are inexperienced or have flown birds your entire life, a Harris's hawk is an exciting and extremely versatile bird of prey to

fly. Harris's hawks are very intelligent birds and, due to their sociable nature, they are easily trainable if you have the right mentor and know what you are doing. They can be very vocal in captivity, as they will see you as a pack member and will call out to you if they can see you. This happens regardless of how they were raised; even quiet Harris's hawks will call out to their human guardian around food time as they are anticipating a nice fly and their favourite snack! They do require the companionship and time of their human guardian to stop them getting bored and destructive in their aviary.

Their cooperative hunting skills can be used in the field too – it is possible to fly more than one Harris's hawk together, even if they have not been raised with the other birds. Again, this makes them very attractive for falconry, as people can all fly their birds together without having to wait for a bird to be called to the glove before letting another fly free.

Intelligent, sociable, good-natured and capable of hunting most prey that a falconer would like to catch, the Harris's hawk is one of the best birds for use in falconry. It will stay tame and bonded to you throughout its life and will fly over most terrains due to its fast and soaring flying style.

Goshawk (*Accipiter gentilis*)

There are now considered to be two separate subspecies of goshawks – the northern goshawk, which is widespread across Europe and Asia, and the American goshawk, which is found in the US and Canada. Goshawks are a large species of true hawk, or *Accipiter*, and have been extensively used in falconry across the world since ancient times.

Goshawks can vary massively in size between the sexes: males are usually between 624g and 737g (1lb 6oz–1lb 10oz) and females can range from 1kg to 1.8kg (2lb 5oz–4lb) in some individuals. They have a wingspan that ranges from 120cm to 165cm (4ft–5.5ft).

Traditionally, Goshawks were used by falconers to hunt game birds such as pheasants, grouse, ducks and geese, as well as ground prey such as rabbits and hares.

Adult birds have a striking colouration: they are a dark slate grey on their backs with a very conspicuous dark grey stripe that runs across their eyes. On the chest, a goshawk is white with dark barring that runs right the way down from the chest to the underside of

Opposite: COMING IN TO LAND
Northern goshawk, *Accipiter gentilis*, coming in for landing.

GOSHAWK EYES
Goshawks are 'true hawks' and will readily hunt a variety of game. Their eye colour can vary from deep red to orange or yellow, depending on the age and sex of the bird.

the tail. Goshawks have stocky, compact bodies, long muscular legs and a very long tail, which they use as a rudder to manoeuvre around trees in the forests that they like to call home.

Naturally, the goshawk is an extremely shy and highly strung character – they are nervous around people in the wild and choose to hide away in thick forests waiting to seek out their next meal.

Goshawks are solitary and independent, so this can make them quite hard to tame in captivity. You will need to spend a lot of time manning the bird on a daily basis to get the best out of their character. They are, however, tenacious hunting birds and are a very traditional bird of prey used in falconry because of their unrivalled success out in the field, but they require more time from the falconer than other species of raptors that are available in captivity.

Peregrine falcon (*Falco peregrinus*)

The fastest animal ever to have lived on Earth with a top speed of over 320km/h (200mph), the peregrine falcon is an incredible, dynamic raptor that specializes in catching other birds in flight. The peregrine falcon will gain height and try to get the advantage of surprise over their prey – when they have spotted a potential food source below them, the peregrine will fold their wings to their side and drop like a bullet from the sky in the form of a high-speed 'stoop' during which they reach record-breaking speeds. They will then strike the prey at full speed, hitting them out of the sky with a strong back talon called the hallux, with the aim of decapitating or killing the prey on impact. The peregrine falcon will then descend and eat the kill on the ground.

The peregrine falcon is a large, powerful bird with a weight range of 510g to 1kg (1lb 2oz–2lb 5oz) and a wingspan of 75–120cm (2.5–4ft). They are a dark slate grey/blue down their back and tail with a pale, cream-coloured chest and legs. They have beautiful, dark brown or black barring that runs down the length of their chest and underbelly. Peregrine falcons have an unmistakeable dark-coloured 'hood' marking that runs down from their beak to underneath their eyes. This helps to reduce the glare of the sun so that the

DESERT FALCON
A gyrfalcon (*Falco rusticolus*),
telemetry attached, flies towards
his trainer in Dubai.

peregrine can fly into the sun and try to get the better of its dazzled prey.

This species is common and widespread across the world – they are found on every continent other than Antarctica and are thriving in the wild. They did become extremely rare in the UK due to the use of pesticides that contained DDT, which weakened the egg shells and therefore meant that the peregrine falcon could not breed successfully. Thankfully, with the banning of these pesticides, the peregrine falcon made a significant comeback and is once again a familiar sight in both cities and the countryside across Britain.

Peregrine falcons eat pigeons, pheasants, ducks and all manner of medium-sized and large birds. On occasion, they will hunt mammals on the ground, although this is extremely rare, as they prefer to hunt flying quarry. With such a different flying style from some other raptors, these falcons are highly prized for falconry in areas that have large, open landscapes that only a high-speed raptor can cover efficiently. Deserts, tundra, open fields and meadow areas – these are the environments in which a falcon will thrive.

Saker falcon (*Falco cherrug*)
This is a very large, brown-and-cream-coloured falcon that is used extensively for falconry in the Middle East, as they are superb hunters over large expanses of flat ground. They can also be found in Eastern Europe, China and Mongolia. However, sadly, they are an extremely rare sight due to this species massively declining in population in the wild over the last few decades. Habitat loss, pesticides and human interference have spelled disaster for breeding pairs of saker falcons in the wild and there are now believed to be only 8,000 to 17,000 pairs in the entire world. They are a target for the illegal falconry trade in the Middle East and eggs are regularly stolen from wild birds so that they can be sold on the falconry market.

There are breeding and conservation projects currently being organized for captive falconry birds to help preserve this beautiful species of raptor and make it less desirable to take the eggs from the wild.

Saker falcons are the second-largest species of falcon, with a weight of between 680g and 1.5kg (1lb 8oz–3lb 5oz) and a wingspan of 110–130cm (3.5–4ft), topped only in size by the closely related gyrfalcon. This means they can catch a huge variety of prey: voles, hamsters, rabbits, hares, pheasants, grouse and large rodents.

Unlike other falcons, the saker prefers to hunt animals on the ground and will therefore fly more slowly and horizontally over large expanses of open ground in order to spot and then swoop down on the unsuspecting target.

Opposite:
'DUCK HAWK'
An adult peregrine falcon, also known as a 'Duck Hawk', in full flight, at Torrey Pines State Natural Reserve, San Diego, California.

Right:
BIG FALCON
The Saker falcon, *Falco cherrug*, is the second-largest species of falcon. Native to Eastern Europe, the Middle East, China and Mongolia, the Saker is in decline, but is the subject of some breeding and conservation projects to change this.

CHOOSING A BIRD OF PREY

Versatile, large and generally a very calm and obedient bird of prey in captivity, it is easy to see why they are one of the most revered and popular falcons used in falconry today. They do require large expanses of land to get the best out of their flying and hunting styles, but they are extremely efficient hunters and very exciting to fly out in the field.

Golden eagle (*Aquila chrysaetos*)
An iconic and powerful bird, the golden eagle is found across North America, Europe, Africa and Asia. They are incredibly fast and have been known to reach speeds of over 160km/h (100mph) as they dive from great heights to pursue and catch prey on the ground.

The golden eagle is a very large species of raptor with a weight of between 2.7kg and 6.4kg (6–14lb) and a wingspan of 180–230cm (6–7.5ft); in flight, they look very striking with their enormous, broad wings extended, showing the typical eagle 'fingertip' primary feathers on the end of their wings and a strong, thickset body with a broad, square tail. Golden eagles are a uniform dark brown colour across their body with light, golden-coloured feathers on their nape and shoulders. Adult birds have a distinct white base to their tail, which can easily been seen in flight or when at rest on the ground. The talons and feet are strong and large; they enable the golden eagle to catch a huge variety of prey including reptiles, fish, rabbits, hares, foxes and even deer.

They have large territories in the wild and one pair of golden eagles can defend a breeding area of around 155km² (60 square miles). This is an eagle of open lands, coasts, forests and mountains – their large size makes it almost impossible for them to navigate around urban areas and they are naturally a very shy species of bird that will choose to be away from humans if at all possible.

If you are choosing to hunt with a golden eagle, you must make sure that you have the space required to fly them free properly, are away from the general public and have plenty of quarry for your eagle to chase.

Right: GOLDEN EAGLE FESTIVAL
The Golden eagle festival in Mongolia is an event where eagle hunters from around Mongolia, known as *berkutchi*, show off their skills competitively. The *berkutchi* not only a role, but a rite of passage.

56

'KING OF THE BIRDS'
The golden eagle, *Aquila chrysaetos*, is a wonderfully majestic, if incredibly shy, species of bird.

CHOOSING A BIRD OF PREY

Barn owl (*Tyto alba*)

The barn owl is a beautiful, medium-sized owl that is almost unmistakeable in appearance due to its pale white and golden plumage. The barn owl is widespread and common throughout the world; they are found on every continent apart from the poles and they prefer to live in countryside and farmland areas where they have the best opportunity to catch their favourite prey: small rodents like mice, voles and shrews.

The barn owl is predominantly pale in colouration on the face and underside, with a golden or buff colour on the back and wings. They have a very distinctive heart-shaped facial disc, which helps them to magnify the sound-waves given off from whatever they are hunting so that they can locate and pinpoint their prey in total darkness. Males are usually pure white down the front of their bodies and under their wings, whereas female barn owls usually have little chocolate-coloured spots in these areas.

Barn owls have a very loud, screeching call, which they will make all night as part of territorial and courtship displays. They are extremely aggressive around their territories in both the wild and captivity.

They are not a particularly large bird and so are very unsuitable for the novice bird of prey trainer, as there is an extremely high risk of losing the bird through poor weight management. Barn owls only weigh between 270g and 350g (9.8–12.5oz) and require a lot of care in the winter months to help them survive cold snaps. If you fail to give them enough food, you can kill a barn owl overnight, just to give you some warning about how delicate they can be.

They have a wingspan of around 90cm (3ft), which is fairly large for the size of the body – this is so the barn owl can beat its wings fewer times while still propelling itself efficiently through the air; by beating its wings less, the barn owl minimizes the risk of being heard and spotted while out hunting. The barn owl has extremely soft feathers to make it completely silent while flying and, as they are a mainly nocturnal species, they are most active and vocal at night even in captivity.

Eurasian eagle owl (*Bubo bubo*)

One of the largest species of owls in the world, the Eurasian eagle owl is an incredibly powerful and beautiful owl that can be found across Europe, Northern Africa and Asia. Eurasian eagle owls prefer to live around coastal regions, forests and large areas of open land such as steppes and grassland.

Eurasian eagle owls are a mottled, dark brown colour across their entire body and they are easily recognizable even at a long distance by the feather tufts on the top of their head and their striking orange eyes. They have more of a round facial disc than the barn owl and extremely large, powerful feet that are feathered right the way down the legs and toes.

In size and weight, the Eurasian eagle owl tops most other species of owls; they have a wingspan of between 165cm and 200cm (5.5–6.5ft) and can weigh from 1.4kg to 4kg (3–9lb). Surprisingly, they are extremely buoyant in flight and will beat their large, broad wings slowly and deliberately to cover large areas of their territory and hunting grounds with ease and speed.

Eurasian eagle owls are classified as apex predators; this means that nothing hunts them other than humans. They are a confident and potentially dangerous owl in captivity due to their size and power but, for flying free, they are actually very good for a novice trainer, as they do have significant ranges in their flying weights, so you are less likely to lose the bird through poor weight management in the early stages of training your eagle owl.

Having a versatile diet means that the Eurasian eagle owl is a very successful predator – it will hunt anything from small rodents, carrion, birds, rabbits and hares up to foxes and even small species of deer. They are mainly nocturnal and crepuscular, meaning that they prefer to hunt either at night or at dawn and dusk when their prey is just emerging from sleep. Eurasian eagle owls are one of a few species of owls that a bird of prey trainer can successfully train to hunt, and they are extremely long-lived in captivity – it is not unusual for this species to have a life expectancy of around 40 years in captivity and 20 years in the wild. They are definitely a long-term commitment but can make a very enjoyable flying and even hunting companion if you are willing to put the time and effort into their training.

Opposite: PEEKABOO
Barn owls, *Tyto alba*, are truly stunning with their heart-shaped facial discs.

APEX PREDATOR
Eurasian eagle owls, *Bubo bubo*, are apex predators capable of taking down small deer.

EYE COLOUR
Eurasian eagle owls have dark ear tufts, whitish eyebrows and orange-red eyes.

PRACTICAL FALCONRY

THE FOUNDATIONS OF TRAINING YOUR BIRD

PRACTICAL FALCONRY

There are different names for a bird of prey at different stages of its life:
• A young bird of prey is called an 'eyass'.
• A juvenile raptor in the first year of its life is called a 'passager'.
• An older bird of prey that has matured beyond its first year is called a 'haggard'.

Flying weight
The flying weight is the foundation of falconry. There are many misconceptions about the flying weight; some people think it is the starvation of a raptor to get the bird to do what the handler wants, but this simply couldn't be further from the truth. As a falconer, the bird's welfare is your greatest concern – you need a happy, healthy and fit raptor or it will become ill, won't hunt and will eventually die or just fly away. After all, why would any bird stay in a situation where it is permanently hungry and mistreated?

The flying weight is the most effective way of maintaining the condition of your bird without the fear of losing it when you fly it free.

An overweight bird of prey will naturally want to sit very still, hide away and not be bothered by anything. In the wild, raptors do not fly for fun; rather, they fly to hunt food for themselves and their offspring as well as for courtship performances and, on occasion, migrations to look for more suitable hunting grounds. Because flying for a bird of prey is very much a practical mode of transport, when they do not need to fly they simply do not move at all. Birds of prey can stay in one position for over three days and not move a muscle. It's in their best interest to do this; other predators and corvids can represent a real danger for birds of prey so if their bellies

Opposite: SOLITARY FLYER
Common buzzard, *Buteo buteo*, in flight. Europe's most common bird of prey are solitary, but known to occasionally work with others.

Below: URBAN BIRD
The African spotted eagle owl, *Bubo africanus*, is frequently considered an 'urban' bird, due to its tendency to nest in close proximity to humans.

are full, they are going nowhere and remaining hidden. When you translate this into falconry, an overweight bird wouldn't feel the need or want to return to you for a potentially long period of time. You would have to wait until the bird is motivated by food again before it will fly back to you.

At the other end of the scale is a starving bird of prey. If a raptor is too low in weight, the bird will lack energy and therefore will not be able to fly over much distance, if at all. They will flap their wings and simply fall to the floor as their energy levels dry up and the engines of flight shut down. Raptors that are too low in weight will die through poor condition; they will be more susceptible to illness and a sudden change in weather could be enough to kill the bird – it really is on a knife edge. It is completely unacceptable and unnecessary to starve any animal, and birds of prey in falconry are no exception. No falconer in the world would ever starve a bird of prey, as it simply won't be able to fly or hunt and would eventually die.

The flying weight, therefore, is the optimum weight that your bird of prey will fly free at so that it has all the energy, fitness and condition it needs to fly like a wild bird without the worry that it might sit in a tree for days on end or experience ill health through low condition.

As a rule of thumb, the smaller the bird of prey, the easier it is to kill through poor weight management. A barn owl, for example, can have a fat weight of 340g (12oz), a flying weight of 326g (11.5oz) and a starving weight of 312g (11oz). So you only have 28g (1oz) between an overweight bird that will be unresponsive to you in the field and a starving bird that, in a cold snap, could pass away overnight. Please note also that these weights are an example and are not to be applied as an accurate weight for any particular barn owl.

A larger bird of prey will have far more room either side of the fat and starving weights to get a good, consistent flying weight, as their body mass can absorb more difference in weight either way. As a beginner, it is therefore better to go for a medium-sized raptor than a small raptor, so that you do not inadvertently kill or lose the bird through poor weight management.

Falconer's knot
One of the first things that you will learn as a falconer is the 'falconer's knot' – a knot that can be tied and untied with one hand.

Above: SAFETY POSITION
A falconer holds an owl in safety position, leash tied to glove.

This quick-release knot features a safety catch to ensure that the bird of prey cannot undo it and escape with its full equipment still attached. Before you get a bird of prey you must learn the falconer's knot, as it is an important safety protocol enabling the falconer to safely tether the bird on a perch or secure it on a glove out in the field.

Moulting
Most birds of prey will moult their feathers during the warmest months of the year. In the wild, they do this because there are more young, inexperienced prey around so having gaps in their feathers does not impede

Opposite: SITTING BIRD
Aplomado falcon, *Falco femoralis*, is native to the southeastern US and South America. It's not unusual for these beautiful birds to pass food to each other in mid-air.

Overleaf: FEEDING
A Ural owl flies in to land on the falconer's glove in this forest winter scene.

Opposite: MOULTING
Juvenile lesser kestrel, *Falco naumanni*, losing its plumage during a moult.

Below: ANKLETS & LEASH
A falcon in safety position wearing anklets and a leash.

their hunting success too much. Birds of prey will usually drop two feathers at a time from their wings and tail and will drop feathers from their body throughout the moult, too. By dropping feathers symmetrically and one by one, they minimize the gaps in their wings and tail and ensure they can continue flying.

In captivity, warmer weather and higher weight are two major components in triggering your bird's moult, so if you'd like to rest your bird throughout the summer months, feed them up to a nice, fat weight and leave them in their aviary so that they can moult their feathers and get ready to fly in the autumn and winter again.

If you would like to fly your bird through the moult, you must still raise their weight to make sure they have enough nutrients and condition to grow new feathers and to trigger the moult initially. Be careful that the bird isn't at a fat weight, though, or you can lose the bird while you are flying it free, as it won't be responsive to food if it is too heavy.

Feathers that are growing through will have blood in the quill/shaft of the feather. It isn't until the feather is fully grown that the blood is stemmed and plugged at the bottom of the shaft and then the quill starts to dry out. While the feather is 'in the blood' it is extremely risky to handle and fly the bird because if the feather snaps, it can bleed out quite heavily and be difficult to stop. Be aware of which feathers are growing through and try to avoid contact with that area until they are 'hard penned' and fully formed.

You can give food supplements to your bird during their moult to help the feathers come through strong and in good condition.

Tethering birds of prey
It goes without saying that a free-lofted bird (kept in an aviary or mews) will live a much happier, healthier life than a bird that is restricted by its legs on a permanent basis by being tied to a perch. There has

Above: IMPRINTING
A Eurasian eagle owl comes in to land on the falconer's glove in a forest.

been extensive medical-based research done in the field of tethered versus free-lofted raptors recently, which shows a significant improvement in health, fitness and behaviour of free-lofted birds when compared with permanently tethered birds.

The modern viewpoint on falconry is that no bird should be permanently tethered. It is seen as completely unethical to do so, and if you do not have the space to build a nice aviary for your bird then you should not use tethering as an option to save on space.

Tethering is, however, absolutely vital for training a young bird and can keep the bird from injuring itself in the initial stages of taming.

There are training methods that do not require tethering, where you spend a far longer time period in the enclosure with your bird; you try to entice it with food to come closer to you, and then you can jump the bird to your glove when it has got used to you being around.

The reason that falconers usually use the tethering method in the initial stages of training is because you can tame the bird in a fraction of the time the free-lofting training method takes. Although initially the tethering training is stressful for the bird, after a couple of weeks they are no longer in that fearful frame of mind and are moving on to the next stages of free flight training, whereas entering an enclosure over a longer period of time can elongate the stress to the bird with little to no benefits over the tethering method. It must also be said that if you free-loft an untrained bird of prey into an aviary, you run the risk of the bird slamming into the sides and roof to get away from you and they can damage their bodies and feathers terribly doing this. We have seen broken beaks, split skin, eye damage, broken feathers and even broken necks in birds that have been

PRACTICAL FALCONRY

let loose in an aviary too soon before their training had even been completed and, realistically, most people entering the world of falconry are not going to have the time or members of staff to sit in with their bird to try and entice it to eat for most of the day. If you need to take your bird to the vet or sit your bird down on a perch for any reason, it absolutely must be comfortable being tethered in these situations.

So use tethering sensibly; aim to tether your bird only when you are going through the initial training process and let the bird free into its aviary as soon as possible.

Below: CRÈCHE REARED
Three young barn owl chicks. At just three weeks old, their legs are too weak to hold their bodies up.

Overleaf: PARENT REARED
A mother Eurasian eagle owl feeds her downy chick in the nest.

77

TRAINING YOUR BIRD OF PREY

**MANNING, LURE AND GLOVE TRAINING
USING A HOOD • FREE FLIGHT TRAINING
HUNTING • TRAINING OWLS**

There are several ways to train raptors depending on the species that you choose and, most importantly, the reason why you would like to fly your chosen bird free. For example, if you are hoping to use a raptor to hunt prey for you, then a parent-reared bird is going to be far more successful in the field.

If, however, you would like a bird of prey to fly free as more of a hobby and enjoyable pastime then perhaps a hand-reared owl or buzzard species might be a better option.

Rearing

A lot of time and thought must go into how the bird will be raised and trained, and adequate housing must be provided for the bird. How a bird is housed and kept will vary for each species, as will how the falconer intends to fly the bird; it is, therefore, essential for the falconer to decide which type of bird will suit their lifestyle and needs.

Without a doubt, a parent-reared bird of prey is a better choice than an imprint due to the aggression and noise that can show in the behaviour of an imprint raptor.

It can be incredibly dangerous to imprint eagles because they are notoriously aggressive with their handlers and members of the public if they are hand-reared – remember, a large, powerful bird that has no fear of humans can cause serious damage and injury to people and can kill animals up to the size of medium dogs.

Never contemplate getting an eagle unless you have already experience with smaller species of raptors, and do not fly an eagle in public places where there are lots of people and pets around, as it is irresponsible and completely unfair to run the risk of scaring the general public and bringing the sport of falconry into disrepute.

Below: STEPPE EAGLE IN FLIGHT
The steppe eagle (*Aquila nipalensis*) has a wingspan that is 2.5 times its body length, and able to fly at a speed of 15.6m (51ft) per second when gliding.

TRAINING YOUR BIRD OF PREY

Left: OWL
Owls are ideal birds if the falconer wants to train a bird as a hobby, rather than use it to hunt prey.

Below: GOLDEN EAGLE
Living across the northern hemisphere, the golden eagle (*Aquila chrysaetos*) hunts a variety of prey, mainly hares, rabbits, marmots and other ground squirrels. Eagles should only be reared and trained by experienced falconers who have previous experience of smaller raptors.

TRAINING YOUR BIRD OF PREY

TRAINING YOUR BIRD OF PREY

Left: MANNING
The main task of the falconer is to establish a bond with their bird, so that the bird always feels comfortable in the relationship. This can be achieved through 'manning', or keeping the bird on the glove for an extended period.

Above: FLIGHT DYNAMICS
Golden eagles are unusual in that they often fly in a noticeable dihedral, which means the wings are held in an upturned V shape.

Environmental factors

If you are in a place with lots of open land and a low population and you wish to hunt large game then an eagle could be a great choice, but you would need to have experience with flying raptors beforehand and ideally an experienced mentor regardless of how perfect the environment might be, because an eagle can be a serious safety risk to you if you do not know what you're doing. You are more likely to lose an imprinted bird of prey in the field as it matures, too – because it will see you as a parent instead of a partnership, the young bird will range far and wide looking for a new territory.

So, we will assume that you have picked up a parent-reared bird of prey from a suitable breeder, you have put all of the correct falconry furniture on the bird and you now have a very wild, unimpressed bird of prey tethered to a block or a bow perch, depending on the species of bird you have acquired.

Picking up your bird of prey

During this time, your primary job is to make sure that the bird of prey starts to lose its fear of you and will be comfortable in your presence and calm when sitting on your glove.

To do this, they must start to see you as a food provider so, in these early stages, the bird cannot eat anywhere but on your glove. If the bird is too scared to eat on your glove for the first few days then simply tether the bird back on the perch, walk around them and be in their space several times a day, but do not throw food to try and feed your bird until it's willing to eat on your glove. This is so important and cannot be accelerated – remember, a bird will never starve itself to death and when the urge to eat gets greater, it competes with their fear of you and eventually overrides that fear so the bird will eat on your glove and pay you little attention.

Without a doubt, your new bird of prey will try and bate (fly) away from you – the bird will be absolutely terrified of you and will do everything it can to get as far away from you as possible. This is why at this stage you must make sure that, when you tether the bird to the block or bow perch, you have the leash at the correct length. If it's too long it can dislocate the bird's legs and if it's too short it will mean the bird could damage its tail feathers as it will hit them up against the perch stand.

Make it comfortable
Because you know the young bird will be thrashing around on the floor trying to get away from you, put some nice, soft artificial grass or a blanket or towel down on top of the pea shingle where the perch is placed. This will be much

Below: PLACING JESSES
A Harris's hawk, with a leash tied to a glove's D-ring with a falconer's knot, bates on the glove as a falconer places jesses into safety position.

PICKING UP YOUR BIRD OF PREY

TYING A FALCONER'S KNOT

A falconer's knot can be tied and untied with one hand, ensuring that the bird remains secure at all times.

1. Pass the rope through the ring on the glove or perch. Grip the tail end of the leash between index and middle finger of the right hand in a scissor action (pictured upper left).

2. Hook the thumb over the top of the leash that is being held in the left hand, thread the thumb through the two pieces and lift the thumb upright, creating a D shape.

3. With the index finger, push part (not all) of the tail length through your D shape to create another loop (pictured lower left).

87

4. For added security, grip the tail again between index and middle finger and repeat the process to create a second falconer's knot on the same leash (left). Repeat until satisfied the bird will be unable to undo the knots.

5. Do not pull the whole tail length through. Rather, pass the tail through the loop and pull to create a lock within the knot, so the bird can't just pull on the leash and undo the knot (below).

Above: HARRIS'S HAWK
A Harris's hawk stands securely tied with a falconer's knot to the moveable ring of a bow perch.

kinder on the bird when it is flapping around on the floor and will minimize feathers being broken in these early stages of training.

All of this may seem a bit tough on the bird but falconry is all about getting over the stress period as soon as possible so that the bird can start to calm and tame down quickly. The initial two weeks may seem a bit daunting for the falconer but if you follow the rules of only feeding the bird on your glove and you sit with the bird several times a day throughout this period, you will be surprised how quickly your falcon will come to accept you and then you can start really building on your partnership.

Walk up to your bird but try not to approach them quickly or noisily – you need to keep the stress levels down as much as possible at this stage so be quiet around the bird and do not try to rush anything. Your bird will bate away from you and will continue to flap its wings and pull constantly in the opposite direction from you and will stay at the end of the leash. Slide the leash into your gloved hand while the bird is bating and lift the bird up on to the glove immediately – when the bird is sitting on or around your gloved hand, untie the falconer's knot on its leash, then stand up and tie the bird to your glove for security.

From now on, you will not feed the bird until it is eating from your glove, so offer them big bits of food to entice it to eat. If the bird does not eat, tie it back

PICKING UP YOUR BIRD OF PREY

PICKING UP YOUR BIRD OF PREY

Opposite: SAFETY POSITION
A Harris's hawk stands on a falconer's glove in safety position, ready for training. Tied to the glove with a falconer's knot, safety position is assumed by winding the jesses under the thumb, through the third and fourth fingers on the gloved hand and closing the fist firmly.

Below: A HARRIS'S HAWK BEING MANNED ON THE GLOVE
Although you do not want to touch the feathers on your bird too much, it is essential that your bird is used to being examined over the entire body to keep it calm during vet visits and when changing its equipment. The falconer should get the bird used to touch on the chest, feet and back during the manning process.

on to its perch, walk away and try again in a couple of hours.

Do not bother weighing the bird daily at this time – you would only cause the bird stress, as it won't want to be near you, and therefore would absolutely not sit on the scales for long enough for you to take a weight. Rather, wait until the bird is settled on your glove and has eaten its first meal before taking its initial weight. The weight of a young, parent-reared bird when it first eats on the glove is usually a very good indicator of what its flying weight will be, because it will be very hungry indeed after fighting the urge to eat for a few days, so you can take that as a low weight and build up from there. For example, if a falcon has just started to eat and the next day I weigh the bird at 510g (1lb 2oz), I would write that down as a responsive, low flying weight with the idea to increase that weight as the bird becomes more confident with me.

PICKING UP YOUR BIRD OF PREY

All photographs:
CORRECT HANDLING
& GLOVE DISCIPLINE
This sequence shows how to feed the bird on the glove with the bird in the right handling position.

1. If your bird is happy to eat while on the glove, this is a good indication of it being at a low flying weight. Note this initial weight and build on the manning process from there (right top).

2. Always keep your bird secured on the glove during the training process by tying the leash with a falconer's knot to the glove. The bird should always face towards you when on the gloved hand – do not allow the bird to turn its back on you or sit awkwardly on the glove, as this could break some of its tail and wing feathers (right lower).

PICKING UP YOUR BIRD OF PREY

3. As the bird becomes used to the falconer, it will show little fear towards you and will eagerly await its feeding time (above & right).

PICKING UP YOUR BIRD OF PREY

PICKING UP YOUR BIRD OF PREY

4. Birds of prey will naturally 'mantle' over their food on the glove. They are hiding the food from anything that may wish to steal it from them. Mantling involves the bird dropping its wings either side of the body in a shielding motion and fanning out their tail to disguise the food completely from behind.

PICKING UP YOUR BIRD OF PREY

Right & below: 'BATING'
An untrained bird will 'bate' – or jump and fall off the falconer's glove – during the initial stages of training. Lift the bird up gently from the front or back, whatever you are most comfortable with, and make sure the bird is standing back on the glove facing towards you. Never allow a bird to hang upside down for long periods of time – ensure you rectify the bating immediately.

PICKING UP YOUR BIRD OF PREY

1. Keeping the bird in safety position, untie it from your glove.

2. Feed the leash through the ring of the perch.

3. Thread the thumb through and lift, creating a D shape.

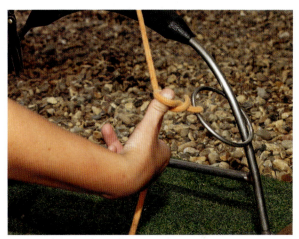

4. Lift the thumb to create D-shaped loop.

5. Pass the tail end through the D shape to create another loop.

6. Extend the loop of the falconer's knot and pass the tail end of the leash through the loop.

97

PICKING UP YOUR BIRD OF PREY

Right & below: TAMING
As your bird becomes more confident with you and starts to tame, it will readily fly to your glove in the aviary (right). Always make sure the jesses are held securely to stop an aggressive hawk from injuring you with a strike with its talons (below).

Opposite all photographs: PICKING UP YOUR BIRD
To pick up your bird, approach from the front and side of the bird so as not to intimidate it by standing directly over it.

PICKING UP YOUR BIRD OF PREY

1. Kneel beside your bird and then reach for the jesses.

2. Grasping the jesses will encourage your bird to step up.

3. Place the jesses in safety position.

4. The bird is now secure on the glove, tied to the perch.

5. Pull the tail end from the falconer's knot.

6. Keep pulling the tail end of the leash to undo the knot.

PICKING UP YOUR BIRD OF PREY

7. Unthread the tail end of the leash from the falconer's knot.

8. Pull on the tail of the leash to undo the falconer's knot.

9. As the tail end of the leash is pulled completely, the knot will unravel.

10. The leash is now untied from the perch and the bird can be picked up safely and secured to the glove.

PICKING UP YOUR BIRD OF PREY

11. Push the tail end of the leash through the glove's D-ring.

12. Tie the falconer's knot to the D-ring to secure the bird.

13. It may feel awkward tying the bird to your glove because you don't have the usual tension on the leash.

PICKING UP YOUR BIRD OF PREY

14. Once you have the correct tension on the leash, you can tie the falconer's knot as previously instructed.

15. Pull the leash through to make a loop in order to secure the falconer's knot.

16. Keep the jesses in safety position at all times when tying or untying the falconer's knot, to ensure the bird doesn't escape.

17. Once the loop has been created, you can feed the tail end of the leash through the loop to create a lock.

PICKING UP YOUR BIRD OF PREY

18. The falconer's knot loop when tied on a glove.

19. Feed the tail end of the leash through the loop to secure and lock the falconer's knot.

20. The final falconer's knot when tied to the glove; you do not need to tie two knots, as you will have the added security of holding the jesses of the bird in safety position while you are handling the bird on the glove.

103

PICKING UP YOUR BIRD OF PREY

All photographs:
WEIGHING YOUR BIRD
It is important to weigh your bird to ensure you're neither under- or over-feeding it. For the bird's comfort, use a modified, digital kitchen scales (left). Turn the scales on and make sure you are weighing the bird in the correct mode: either kilos and grams or pounds and ounces – whatever you prefer. In order for the bird to sit comfortably on the scales while being weighed, use a T perch that has astroturf covering the top bar (below).

104

PICKING UP YOUR BIRD OF PREY

1. Hold the bird with the back of its legs to the perch. It should step backwards on to the scales and always face the falconer.

2. Let the bird settle on to the scales in order to get an accurate weight. Never let the jesses go completely – loosen your grip but still have the leash between your middle and index finger.

3. Lift the jesses and leash so that your bird's weight doesn't include the weight of the swivel (above right).

105

Manning, lure and glove training

The watershed moment for any falconer is when a bird trusts you enough to lower its head and eat the food from your glove. Once you're at this stage of the training process, your bird should come on in leaps and bounds. Let the bird eat as much as it can on this first day so that it gets a huge reward for trusting you and feeding on the glove.

Start weighing the bird every single day
After allowing the bird to gorge on food the previous day, this will obviously push its weight up the following day, so the bird may well be a bit feral when you try to pick it up the next morning but, again, apply the same techniques: pick up the bird from its perch, untie the falconer's knots and tie the bird on to your glove.

Stand up or sit down, it really does not matter – just make sure you're comfortable and that the bird is settled on the glove. Hold a nice, large bit of food in your gloved hand and if the bird does not eat on your glove, put the bird back on its perch, tie the falconer's knot to keep your precious new addition safe from escape, and leave it for the day.

When the bird is starting to feed well from your glove, take it for a walk around your garden so that it can get used to different locations. Only take the bird out in public when it is settled with you – there is nothing worse than seeing a stressed bird hanging upside down on a glove because it's terrified of a noisy or crowded environment. In the initial training stages, it is better to invite your friends over so that the bird can get used to lots of different people in a familiar environment where it won't be too overwhelmed.

Below: FOOD REWARD
Food is the most valued prize for your bird of prey – only feed the bird on your glove during the initial training period.

MANNING, LURE AND GLOVE TRAINING

Left & below: POSITIVE CONDITIONING
You can pass the food to the bird's beak in small pieces as well as putting larger, more highly sought-after rewards on the glove. This will allow the bird to see you as the sole food provider and will make sure the bird views you in a positive way. Always keep the jesses in safety position when feeding your bird, as they can get excited and lash out with their feet in these early training sessions.

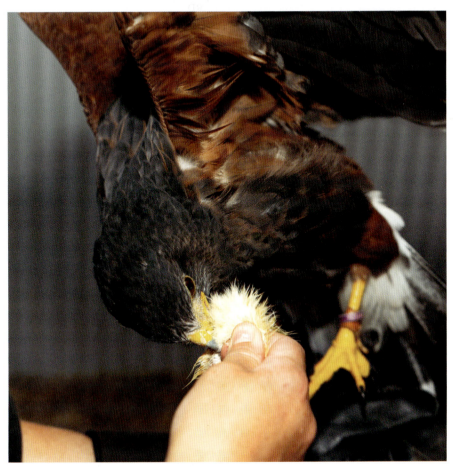

Introducing the hood

Falcons are incredibly sight-driven predators. Any movement will send them over the edge; they are designed to seek out fast-moving prey at a distance and have the most incredible, telescopic vision. To calm a falcon, both in training and when out hunting in the field, it is therefore absolutely essential that you get the falcon used to wearing a hood.

It is a very good idea to get any bird of prey, not just falcons, used to wearing a hood because there may be times when you need to walk the bird through very congested areas or they need to have medical treatment, and a hood will calm the bird greatly in any unsettling, new situation.

Leather hoods are easily available to buy online or at any falconry show, so you by no means have to be a leatherwork master to own a falcon, but hood training is essential. You should never fly a falcon without a hood – if the bird is going to chase a lure for exercise, for example, it will see the lure immediately and bate towards it. If the falcon is being held on the glove by a second person, this can cause damage to the bird's legs if the falcon constantly bates off the glove and is restrained. It is the same if the falconer is walking out over large, open areas where falcons are most often flown at game – the falconer will keep the bird hooded so that it remains calm until a signal is raised that there is suitable prey nearby or something gets flushed so it's a good time to send the falcon up into the air.

Either way, a hood will be used for a falcon throughout its entire life, from training right

Below: FITTING A HOOD (1)
Leather hoods are fitted over the bird's head to keep them calm. They are essential for initial training and come in a variety of different shapes and sizes, depending on the species of bird they will fit.

INTRODUCING THE HOOD

1. The hood is comprised of leather and two sets of braces, which you will use to open and close the hood when it is on the bird (pictured left). A small amount of food has been placed inside the hood to tempt the bird.

2. Take the hood in your right hand and make sure the space for the beak is facing down towards the floor as you start lifting it towards the bird (below).

INTRODUCING THE HOOD

3. Gently raise the hood towards the bird and slide the hood over its beak (above).

4. Your bird may push its head away from the hood but continue to slide it over the beak until the hood is now sitting loosely on the bird's head (right).

5. Take one side of the brace straps in your teeth and the other side in your right hand; now pull together to close the hood securely on the bird's head (opposite).

110

INTRODUCING THE HOOD

up until it is a fully trusted member of your family. As soon as your bird of prey has started eating on the glove, this is the time to introduce the hood.

Sweetening the process

I am all for positive reinforcement as opposed to 'breaking' the bird by forcing a hood on its head, no matter how the bird feels about it, so I have found the best method for hooding any species of bird is to place small bits of food inside the hood by turning it upside down and offering the inside of the hood to the bird. It will see lots of nice things to eat inside the hood and will start dipping its head into the hood to take the food. Do this several times and then lift the hood over the bird's head so that it is fitted without the braces being closed.

Take the hood off and repeat this several times until the bird is comfortable with the hood being put over its head. When the bird is sitting with the hood on more comfortably, you can then close the braces and secure the hood on to its head.

After a few minutes, take the hood off and allow the bird to eat from your glove, so you are reinforcing a positive association of food with wearing a hood. Always hood your bird to weigh it and when you are doing any kind of training.

FITTED HOOD
A Harris's hawk standing on a falconer's glove wearing a leather hood.

INTRODUCING THE HOOD

**Right & below:
FITTING THE HOOD (2)**
Introduce your falcon to the hood by gently pressing the hood on its chest. When the falcon is getting used to the hood, start raising it towards the bird's face.

INTRODUCING THE HOOD

1. Slide the hood over the beak through the hole in the hood.

2. The hood should sit on the falcon's head loosely.

3. Hold the brace straps between your teeth and right hand.

4. Pull together to close the hood on the falcon's head.

5. The straps will close the hood tightly around the bird's head, so that it can't remove it with its feet or when it shakes its head.

6. When the hood is fully fitted, make sure the bird is sitting comfortably on your glove to minimize the bird trying to bate.

INTRODUCING THE HOOD

SITTING CALMLY
Your falcon will sit calmly on the glove now until you remove the hood and start the training session.

Recall training

Manning, socializing and getting your bird tame are the most integral foundations for falconry. When the bird is feeding and sitting on your glove nicely, used to different locations, not showing fear of strange people, animals or environments, and not bating away from you when you walk into its aviary, you are ready to let the bird loose in its enclosure.

Attaching flying jesses
Take off the jesses, swivel and leash so that they can't get caught on anything in the aviary and replace them with flying jesses so that you can still hold the bird in an emergency situation if required. Let the bird go free in the aviary and explore its new surroundings.

Above: FLYING JESSES
Examples of leather flying jesses.

Every morning, call your bird to the glove, take up the flying jesses in your hand, hood your falcon and weigh the bird.

Weighing your bird
You now need to work out your bird's flying weight, so monitor at which weights the bird is most responsive to flying to your glove and take these weights as a starting point for what you would like the bird to weigh when you start the outside flying training. Write down the bird's behaviour and responsiveness to each weight so that you can start to get an idea about the weights that are working for your bird.

Take off the hood after weighing the bird, let the bird go free in its enclosure, and start to jump the bird to your gloved hand for food,

Above: BRAIDED JESSE
Examples of braided rope jesses.

RECALL TRAINING

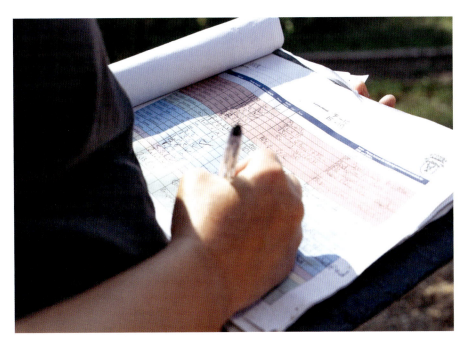

Left: RECORDING
Documenting details of a bird's weight, behaviour and responsiveness is a key part of falcon care.

Below: LURE
A lure pad attached to a length of rope with a handle for the falconer to keep hold of during use.

RECALL TRAINING

Above, left & opposite:
ATTACHING A CREANCE
1. You must attach the creance to the swivel. You only take the leash off your bird and replace it with the creance – no other falconry furniture will be removed at this point (above).

2. Depending on the swivel type, you should be able to tie the usual falconer's knot to the end of the metal swivel (left); undo the clip-style swivel that is attached to the leash and remove it from the jesses altogether.

RECALL TRAINING

3. This creance is attached to another swivel and is simply clipped on to the jesses in place of a leash. The creance is now attached to the jesses via the swivel (above).

which is the first part of its recall training. Cut the large bits of food that you have been feeding the bird into lots of smaller bits so that the bird is still eating the same amount but is having to fly to your glove multiple times to get it. This will be a new, exciting game for the bird and it will start pre-empting your glove being raised so that it can eagerly fly towards you and get a little reward.

Outside training

After a few days of successfully flying the bird to your glove in the aviary, it is time to attach the creance to your bird and take it to a safe area where you will teach it to fly to your glove, continuing the same training outside. Hood your bird, put the mews jesses, swivel and leash back on the bird in its aviary and weigh your bird. Mark down the weight and how much food you are going to feed it that day.

When you are in your outside training area, take off the leash and fit the creance to where the leash was. It is very important to secure the other end of the creance to either a post or yourself or, ideally, have a friend go with you so that they can hold on to the handle of the creance and keep control of the bird just in case it decides to bolt during the training session.

All birds of prey react differently when they are first taken out into a field or any outside environment; they can feel the wind under their wings, there are other birds and animals around and their natural instinct to want

RECALL TRAINING

Right: SAFETY POSITION
A hooded falcon is held in safety position on a glove in preparation for recall training.

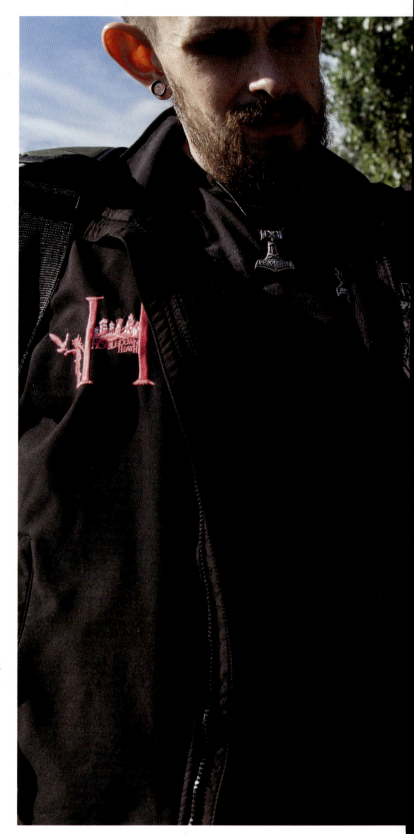

to fly will kick in almost immediately. That's why in the first few outings, you must keep the creance very short – about 1m (3.3ft) is all that's needed, as you want the bird to focus on you and jump to your glove for its food despite all the distractions.

When you are ready and have your bird in position, unhood your bird and try to get it to jump just a few inches to your glove over the first few training sessions to smaller bits of food that make up its total meal for the day. If the bird does not respond and is too distracted by everything around it, do not feed the bird that day; pick the bird up, put the hood back on, reattach the mews jesses, swivel and leash and take the bird home. From now on, your bird won't get fed until it is jumping to your glove outside.

Establishing a flying weight
The next morning, take a note of your bird's weight (it will be lower if it didn't eat the previous day) and then see how the bird reacts out in the field at a lower weight. Birds can sometimes go three days without eating in these early stages of training, so please do not worry about the bird getting too low in weight – as soon as the bird is hungry enough, it will focus on you and get a food reward. Mark the weight at which the bird is jumping to you now as a potential flying weight and repeat this process until the bird is flying the full length of the creance to your gloved hand.

It is at this point that you will introduce the lure to your falcon if you have chosen this particular species of raptor to train.

122

RECALL TRAINING

RECALL TRAINING

FOOD REWARD
Rewarding the bird for its success promotes trust and understanding between bird and trainer.

Lure training

Falcons are usually trained to chase or come back to a lure, because it replicates fast-moving prey that the bird will naturally love to hunt. Even in the field when out hunting with a falcon, the falconer will always have a lure to entice the bird back to where they're standing after the falcon has been off chasing prey. It is a very effective tool and a fun thing for a falcon to interact with, so it is integral in a falcon's training to introduce the lure as soon as possible.

It is very important to get your falcon flying to your glove, as they will be returning to your glove after they have caught the lure. Therefore, do not skip the glove work and go straight to throwing a lure on the ground, since it can be difficult to train the bird to come back to your glove if you do this.

Training steps

Tie a large piece of food on to the lure pad and just drop it on the floor in front of your falcon and unhood the bird; your falcon (still on the creance) will no doubt jump straight on to the lure pad and start eating the food on the floor but, if it hesitates, you can always wiggle the lure with the rope that's attached to it (that you or a friend will be holding). That should motivate the falcon to jump on to the lure pad, bind with it and start eating.

When the falcon has finished eating the food on the lure, kneel down next to the bird and offer it the rest of its food on your glove and call the bird to your glove from the lure. The falcon should jump up nicely and start feeding on your glove; you can then hood your bird after it has eaten and put the lure pad away ready for tomorrow's training.

Below: TEAMWORK
It's much easier to have someone else hold the falcon on their glove when you are initially training your falcon. This allows you to control the creance while you get the bird used to the lure.

LURE TRAINING

All photographs: LURE TRAINING
1. When you are in position with the lure and the creance is secured to you, the hood can be removed from the falcon (left).

2. Allow the falcon to see the lure on the floor – you can drag the lure a little bit to get the bird's attention (below).

LURE TRAINING

3. When your falcon is about to take flight, they will open their wings and bob their head to indicate that they are focused on the lure (above).

4. If the falcon isn't initially interested in the lure on the ground, lift the lure off the ground and hold it up in mid-air (left).

5. When the lure is hanging in mid-air, it allows for more movement on the lure pad, and this should get your falcon's attention (opposite top).

LURE TRAINING

Repeat exercise
Over the next few days, you will tie the creance on to your falcon, hood the bird every time you go outside with it and only take the hood off when the lure is in position. Sit the bird down on whatever perch you have been using outside (or, ideally, a friend who can hold the falcon on their glove at a distance). You will be dropping the lure pad on to the ground at longer and longer distances so that the falcon is flying directly to the lure, eating and then jumping to your glove for the rest of its food.

If you do not have someone who can help you to unhood the bird when the lure is in position, you will have to run with the lure after unhooding the bird to get the same effect.

When the falcon has got the hang of seeking out the lure pad, you can then hold the lure up in the air so that the next time the falcon wants to grab the lure, it has to do so in mid-air and then bring it to the ground to feed. Repeat the process of calling the falcon to the glove and keep doing this routine until you are comfortable that, when the falcon is released, the bird will head directly towards the lure, catch it and feed from it.

Next steps
When the bird is consistently flying at the same weight, you have worked out how much food you need to feed your falcon to maintain that weight and you are happy that the bird is responsive both to your glove and to the lure pad, you can let the bird fly free.

LURE TRAINING

6. Hold the lure in the air until your falcon is interested enough to take flight towards it (left).

7. The falcon will fly towards the lure while it is being held in mid-air (below).

8. You are aiming for the falcon to strike at the lure pad – drop the lure pad as soon as the bird has hit it and locked on to it with their feet (opposite).

LURE TRAINING

LURE TRAINING

9. The falcon will start to eat the food on the lure pad as soon as it feels comfortable to do so (opposite).

10. When the falcon has finished eating it will naturally look for more food – be ready and have the rest of the food on your glove so that the falcon can see it immediately (left).

11. Call the falcon to your glove – you can tap your glove or whistle to get the bird used to looking for the glove from the lure (bottom).

133

LURE TRAINING

12. When the falcon has returned to the glove and eaten all of the food, you can now put the hood back on the bird. This is another positive reinforcement to the hood (above).

13. Slide the hood over the bird's beak when it is settled on the glove (left).

LURE TRAINING

14. Make sure the hood is sitting comfortably on the falcon's head (above).

15. Pull the braces to close the hood around the bird's head (left).

LURE TRAINING

GAME TIME
Your falcon will start to see the lure training as a fun game – here a peregrine hybrid is chasing the lure in free flight.

Free Flight Training

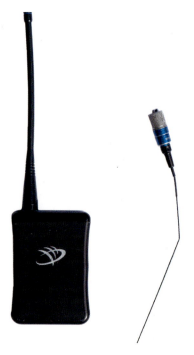

Before you fly your bird of prey free, weigh the bird and make sure you are happy that it's at a weight where it has been very responsive. Hood your bird as you would every day and make sure that it is only wearing flying jesses so that it won't get caught up in a tree should it decide to make an exit from the training area.

Attach the telemetry equipment to your bird and make sure that you have full battery power in both the transmitter and receiver, whether you are using GPS or radio telemetry. Check the telemetry is working and on the right channels before you let the bird go. Remember: telemetry is the only way you can guarantee that you will find your bird if it gets lost – never fly any bird without telemetry.

Unhood your bird and place them on the same perch in the familiar, outside training area that you have been using previously.

Above: TELEMETRY EQUIPMENT
GPS tracker and pocket link telemetry system.

All photographs: USING TELEMETRY
1. Turn on the pocket link using a magnet – this will search for any nearby GPS transmitters.

FREE FLIGHT TRAINING

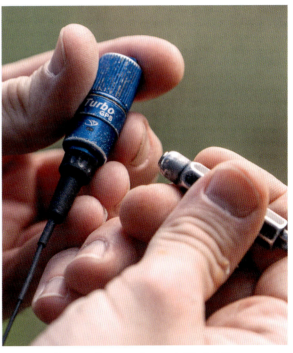

2. Touch the magnet on to the top of the pocket link to activate it.

3. You can also turn the transmitter on/off by holding a magnet up against it. Just touch the magnet on to the transmitter and the light will start blinking when it is switched on.

4. If you have GPS telemetry, you will usually be given access to whatever app they are using to track your bird (left). Always make sure you can see your bird on the tracking software before you let the bird fly free.

FREE FLIGHT TRAINING

All photographs:
BIRD CARRIER
Bird carriers are dark, ventilated spaces that allow the bird to be transported in peace and security.

1. The bird's leash stays on them in the carrier, tied with a falconer's knot to the door for safety (above).

2. Once at your location, untie the falconer's knot from the door. For now, keep the door closed (left).

FREE FLIGHT TRAINING

3. Tie the leash to your glove's D-ring, then open the door (above left).

4. Allow your bird to come to your glove (above right).

If the bird you are training is a falcon: show your falcon the lure and, on the first day of flying the falcon free, just allow the bird to fly to the lure straight away, eat and then return to your glove. Hood your falcon after the bird has eaten all of its food, and celebrate! Your bird is now flying free.

Manipulating the lure

Over the next few training sessions, when you are happy that the bird is flying consistently to the lure, you can start pulling the lure away from the falcon as it starts to dive in on the lure pad, and swing the lure as the bird passes you. This will instantly fire up the falcon's desire to chase its food, so the bird will be looking back at you and then should turn towards you again and start aiming for the lure pad. I would always keep these early lure-chasing games short and sweet.

Aim for two or three passes, and then shout or whistle a command to the falcon that shows the bird that you are going to give it the lure – we usually blow a whistle, then, when the falcon is coming towards us, we throw the lure into the air so that the bird can catch it and bring it to the floor.

Build on this exercise over time, and soon your falcon will be chasing the lure several times in a row and will really start to build up its muscle tone. As this happens, you may have to raise the bird's weight substantially from your initial flying weight, so go by how the bird is behaving and, if the bird seems really hungry, feed it more and see how the falcon performs at a higher weight.

Food reward

If your bird is any species other than a falcon and you are not using a lure to train the bird, show your bird a nice food reward on your glove and only ask it to jump to your glove over a small distance; a few inches is absolutely fine at this stage.

If the bird is happy to jump a few inches, place the bird back on to its original perch and then take a step

FREE FLIGHT TRAINING

All photographs:
FREE FLIGHT TRAINING
1. Prepare your telemetry transmitter, ready to be attached to your bird's equipment. In this example, we use cable ties (left).

2. Thread the cable tie through the anklet's eyelet (below).

FREE FLIGHT TRAINING

back from your original location so that you're asking the bird to jump longer and longer distances.

Keep the initial free flying session very short – I would ask the bird to fly to my glove a maximum of five times at this stage, because as the hawk is taking in food, you could find the bird getting more and more distracted and less interested in you.

Always reward the bird on the final flight with a large piece of food; put the jesses, swivel and leash back on the hawk while it is feeding on your glove.

Building exercise
Build on this exercise and soon your hawk will really start to build up its muscle tone. You can walk away from the hawk to encourage it to follow you and try to find a better vantage point in front of you.

Eagles will behave in a very similar fashion to falcons at this point – our eagles shoot past us and gain height rapidly, then they soar on the thermals above us, waiting for us to either call them to our glove or flush something that they can catch below.

3. Carefully complete the cable tie's circuit (above).

4. Tighten the cable tie until it fits snugly against the eyelet. Remember that the bird doesn't wear mews jesses when free flying, in case the bird gets caught via the jesses' holes. The same principle applies when deciding how much to tighten the cable tie (below).

143

FREE FLIGHT TRAINING

5. Trim off the ends of the cable tie once secured, for the bird's ease and comfort.

6. Your bird is now prepared with telemetry.

Eagles are usually flown from the fist when they are out hunting in the field and it is strongly recommended that you hood an eagle if you are going to start catching prey with them, as it keeps them calm and focused on a long day of hunting.

Goshawks

It must be noted that, although the training process is the same for a goshawk, it is not advisable to let them go off into the trees and ask them to follow you as you would for a Harris's hawk or buzzard. Goshawks require constant interest to keep them focused on the handler, so most people who fly goshawks will hood them when they are walking with the bird on the glove and will only unhood the bird and let them go in the field if prey has been flushed/sighted.

If the goshawk misses the prey, the falconer will then give an immediate command to the goshawk to recall the bird to the glove. If you try to let the goshawk free-range too much, you run the risk that it will start chasing everything in sight and lose interest in you, and then it is extremely likely that you will lose your bird to the wild.

Raising weight

As with all trained raptors, you may have to raise the bird's weight substantially from your initial flying weight so go by how the bird is behaving and if the bird seems really hungry, feed it more and see how the hawk performs at a higher weight.

7. With the bird in safety position, you can now remove your bird's swivel.

144

FREE FLIGHT TRAINING

8. Start removing the swivel but always hold your bird in safety position until you are ready to let it fly free.

9. Take the swivel off both jesses and if you need to, fit the flying jesses once the swivel has been removed. This is an example of a clip swivel, which is attached to permanent flying jesses, so they do not need to be replaced.

10. Now free from the leash and fitted with flying jesses and telemetry, walk with your bird to where you feel it would be best and safest to fly it.

FREE FLIGHT TRAINING

11. Open up your hand to release the jesses from safety position (left).

12. Release your bird. If required, you may also untie the leash from your glove for now (below).

13. Your bird will be excited to fly free – keep their interest by recalling them back to your glove for food several times within the free flight period (opposite top).

14. Always fly the bird to the back of your hand to avoid any injury (opposite bottom).

148

FREE FLIGHT TRAINING

FREE FLIGHT TRAINING

**All photographs:
TYING A LEASH**
1. Tie the leash back to your glove while your gloved hand holds the leash and swivel. This will help you work out how much slack is needed for when you want to put the swivels back on the bird (left).

2. Pull your thumb back to make a D shape (below).

3. Pass the tail end of the leash through the D shape (opposite top).

4. Pull through to make a loop (opposite below).

FREE FLIGHT TRAINING

FREE FLIGHT TRAINING

5. Extend the loop if necessary to make it easier to pass the remaining leash through (right top).

6. Pass the tail end of the leash through the loop (right below).

FREE FLIGHT TRAINING

7. The tail of the leash will now create a lock that the bird of prey can't untie (above).

8. Pull to tighten the falconer's knot (left).

FREE FLIGHT TRAINING

9. Re-attach the swivel to your bird's jesses while it eats from your glove (right).

10. Rewarding your bird for excellent flying is always a great idea. Make sure you have a large piece of food for them to eat at the end of the free flight session. Hold your bird in safety position at all times – they will become quite agitated over food and could cause an injury to the falconer with their feet if they lash out (below & opposite).

FREE FLIGHT TRAINING

Hunting training

Falcons take to catching live prey very easily – they are used to chasing the lure pad and will view most things in the air as potential prey.

As falcons are long-winged, fast-flying birds, you will need a very large area of open ground to hunt with a falcon successfully. A lot of falconers use dogs to locate quarry for the falcon when they are out in the field to keep the bird focused and have more successful slips at the prey.

A falcon will usually 'wait on' (hover) above the falconer – you will let the falcon go from your glove and it will rise up nice and high; the bird will then wait on overhead and is constantly watching what you are doing on the ground. As soon as the prey has been flushed, a falcon will stoop at high speed down towards it and deliver a fatal strike to the animal in mid-air or on the ground. When you collect your bird, allow it to eat some of the kill as a reward and then trade with the bird – give it some food in your glove in exchange for the kill. Hood the falcon and place the kill in your falconry bag – or leave the carcass if you prefer for wildlife to eat it.

Hunting with a hawk, buzzard or eagle

A Harris's hawk, goshawk, golden eagle or red-tailed buzzard will take to hunting very well and with little to no encouragement from

Below: BUILDING A BOND
Continue building up the bond between yourself and the bird of prey once you have trained the bird to fly free. You can now move on to teaching your bird to hunt, if desired.

HUNTING TRAINING

Above & below: USING DIFFERENT PERCHES
Consider flying your bird to different perches within the aviary to make it look for food elsewhere than the glove.

Encourage your bird of prey to look for other locations to land other than your glove, so that it will seek higher perches and different vantage points to land on when you are in the field.

HUNTING TRAINING

**Above & left:
STEPPE EAGLE**
Here a steppe eagle is being encouraged to land on a large, natural perch in his aviary so that he is looking for food around his familiar space. Using small rewards in different places will encourage the bird to focus on their nearby environment as well as the glove.

HUNTING TRAINING

Above: POTENTIAL DANGER
Eagles can be aggressive when you lower their weight and they are seeking out food. Remain vigilant with the larger species of birds during hunting training and always be ready wearing a large glove, so that you can call the bird to you safely and restrain their feet if necessary.

the falconer. They will chase after birds and mammals, will instinctively put a lot of effort into the chases and will learn very quickly how to outsmart their prey.

Other species of buzzards, such as common or ferruginous buzzards, can take a lot more work to get hunting because they are naturally lazier due to their preference of eating carrion in the wild.

Eagles are huge, broad-winged, fast-flying birds and will require vast areas of open land to fly safely and successfully. Hawks and buzzards can be flown at quarry far more easily because they do not require the bigger environments to fly them and, in fact, Harris's hawks in particular do very well flying around towns, cities and suburban areas, where they catch pigeons and small rodents. Ideally, you should have some

woodland or a nice, open farmer's field that you have permission to fly on with some good quarry so that your bird has the best chance of catching something while it is learning how to hunt.

You can start training your hawk, eagle or buzzard to catch prey with a 'dummy bunny', which is like a lure but in the shape of a rabbit. You can attach food to the dummy bunny, drag it along the floor and encourage your bird to chase and lock on to the food. After a while, the bird will start to see small shapes running on the ground as a food source and will therefore more readily chase ground game such as hares and rabbits. I have also known people to just drag a rabbit or pheasant carcass on the ground for their bird to chase and grab on to, which has a high success rate, too.

The species of bird that you are flying, as discussed previously, will decide whether you choose to fly your bird from the glove or to let the bird follow on through the trees when you are out hunting. Hawks, eagles and buzzards will chase their prey quickly over short distances and therefore rely on the element of surprise, either from a vantage point in the trees or by

HUNTING TRAINING

Left & below:
GLOVE RECALL
When out hunting, it is still essential to retain good glove recall in case an unexpected danger or situation presents itself to you while out in the field. Here the steppe eagle is being called to the glove for small food rewards to maintain the bond between the falconer and the bird.

HUNTING TRAINING

Above: EXPERIENCED TRAINER
Eagles are powerful predators and should only be handled by experiences falconers. Make sure you wear an eagle glove to protect you from their strong grip and large talons.

Right: POWERFUL TALONS
Steppe and golden eagles can be trained to hunt rabbits, hares and even small deer. Their feet are large and powerful enough to hold this large quarry when out in the field.

swooping down on the prey from a height. They will grab the prey by the head and body and will hold it on the floor to crush and kill their catch. When you collect your bird from the kill, allow it to eat some of the animal as a reward and then trade with the bird – give it some food in your glove in exchange for the kill. If you have trained your eagle, hawk or buzzard to the hood, this is the time to put the hood back on the bird when it's safely tied to your glove again, and place the kill in your falconry bag or leave the carcass if you prefer for wildlife to eat it.

EAGLE GAUNTLET
A steppe eagle stands comfortably on his handler's leather eagle gauntlet after initial hunting training within the aviary.

HUNTING TRAINING

Right: VANTAGE POINT
Encourage your bird of prey to look for things from different vantage points so that it starts to look beneath where it is perching when out in the field. Here the steppe eagle is being held higher with food being presented on the floor, so that the eagle learns to swoop from a higher vantage point.

Below: SWOOPING
A steppe eagle coming in to land on food. You can use a 'dummy bunny' if you would like your bird to start catching rabbits out in the field.

HUNTING TRAINING

Above: FLYING DISTANCE
Increase both the flying distance to the glove within the hunting training process and the food reward sizes, to keep your bird focused on good glove recall.

Left: FAMILIAR PERCH
Walk around with your bird of prey on the glove within its aviary without food too. This will allow the bird to see you as a convenient perch when out in the field, without the constant expectation that you will feed it. From now on, your bird must look for its own food!

HARRIS'S HAWK
A Harris's hawk flying free in a woodland area with its eyes locked on to potential prey. Harris's hawks are fast, manoeuvrable birds that will catch a large variety of quarry, from partridge, pheasants, rabbits and hares, to ducks and even geese!

OWL TRAINING

The most notable difference between owls and other species of raptors that you find in captivity is that you are more likely to hand-rear or imprint a young owl.

Owlets are usually picked up at around four to six weeks old depending on the species, and they will rely totally on you for food and security until they have all of their adult feathers (hard penned) and can safely be put in their enclosure to fend for themselves and gain a bit of independence.

Imprinting has huge advantages and disadvantages. Obviously, as you are hand-rearing the owlet, it will of course have no fear of you whatsoever and will look to you as its parent and food provider, so training an owl in the early stages can be far easier than a parent-reared bird because the owl is likely to follow you around and be very keen to jump to you for food.

However, this is where a lot of people go wrong – they allow the owlet to jump all over them and even feed the young bird while it's sitting on their shoulder or, even worse, their head. Believe me, this will be absolutely disastrous when the owl is a strong, adult bird and you could sustain serious facial injuries from an over-eager owl that is demanding its dinner if it's been used to being fed near your face.

Imprinted owls are also noisy, so it is not advisable to get one if you are in a built-up area – your neighbours probably won't take too kindly to a nocturnal species of animal making very loud calls all through the night. Owls are also

All photographs: FITTING FLYING JESSES
This Eurasian eagle owl is wearing flying jesses in training.

OWL TRAINING

1. Pick up the owl on your gloved hand. Use food to fly the owl to your glove if required.

2. Keeping the owl on your glove, start threading the flying jess through the anklet with the knot on the outside of the eyelet.

3. Thread the flying jess through the eyelet of the owl's anklet.

4. Pull the jess all the way through the eyelet.

5. Place the jesses into safety position as soon as they have both been fitted, to ensure the bird is secured on the glove.

6. Here, the Eurasian eagle owl is held in safety position on the glove after the flying jesses have been fitted on the anklets.

OWL TRAINING

All photographs: INITIAL FLIGHT TRAINING
1. Show your owl a nice lump of food on your glove – this will garner your bird's interest.

2. Always face the back of your hand to the bird so that it will land with the front of its body facing you. Allow the owl to hop to your glove.

3. Increase the distance gradually to make the jumps more challenging, encouraging the owl to fly to you over longer distances.

OWL TRAINING

4. Always reward your owl with a big piece of food on the glove for the final flight, to make sure that glove work is always a positive interaction.

5. To train your owl to fly to different perches, present food to the bird in front of the perch. This will encourage it to seek out other landing spots.

extremely territorial and may attack you or try to mate with you when you enter their aviary, especially during the breeding season.

Owls can have complicated mood swings and will need your attention and focus for their entire life to keep them flying free well and to keep them calm around people – many owl species can live to over 20 years old, so it is a very long-term commitment. However, if done correctly, you will have a bond with a beautiful bird that gives you lots of enjoyment for many years.

Understanding owl physiology
Owls have an amazing ability to rotate their heads up to 270 degrees, a feature that distinguishes them from many other birds and mammals. This unique capability is primarily due to their specialized skeletal and vascular adaptations, which ensure that blood flow to the brain and eyes is not interrupted during extreme head movements.

The owl's ability to rotate its head that far without incident is a marvel of evolutionary engineering that allows owls to maintain their acute vision and auditory senses while rotating their heads extensively.

Skeletal adaptations
One of the main reasons owls can rotate their heads so far is the structure of their cervical vertebrae. Owls have 14 cervical vertebrae, compared with the seven found in humans. This increased number of vertebrae provides greater flexibility and range of motion. In addition, the joints between these vertebrae are highly specialized. They possess larger, more pivot-like structures called

171

OWL TRAINING

All photographs: ATTACHING THE CREANCE
1. For training outdoors, attach the creance in place of the leash.

2. Hold your owl in safety position. Pass the end of your creance through the swivel.

3. Pull through as you would your bird's leash.

4. Pass the creance through the swivel, keeping the tail to the left.

5. Insert your thumb through the two pieces.

6. Lift your thumb upright, creating a D shape.

OWL TRAINING

7. With index finger, push part of tail length through the D shape.

8. Extend the loop by pulling it out with your index finger

9. Pass the tail through the loop.

10. Feed the rest of the tail through.

11. Pull to create your locked falconer's knot.

12. Pull to secure.

13. With your owl now securely attached to the creance, place small pieces of food on your glove, allowing the owl to make short jumps, gradually increasing distance to allow for short flights to your glove (as above).

14. The owl must land on the glove to claim its reward (right).

OWL TRAINING

'zygapophyses', which afford the bird smoother, more extensive rotational movements. These adaptations enable the owl's neck to support and manoeuvre the head through a broad range of angles without causing injury.

Vascular adaptations

Just as important as the skeletal modifications are the vascular adaptations that ensure a continuous blood supply during head rotation. One critical adaptation is the presence of a vascular network known as the 'carotid and vertebral artery reservoirs'. These reservoirs are found at the base of the owl's head and neck. They allow the owl to store a small amount of blood, which can be used to maintain circulation to the brain, even if some arteries are temporarily constricted or blocked during head rotation.

Owls have unique bone structures in their necks that create 'bony channels' through which the major blood vessels pass. These channels act as protection for the arteries, preventing them from becoming stretched or pinched during the extreme head rotations. Studies have shown that the walls of these arteries are more elastic and capable of handling such movements without tearing or obstructing blood flow.

All photographs: FLYING YOUR OWL FREE
When the owl has been responsive and has been flying to the glove on the creance for at least a week, you can start to fly it free.
1. A Eurasian eagle owl waits on a perch for the handler to show it food (above top).
2. Show your owl a piece of food to get the bird interested and focused on you (above lower).
3. The owl aims lands on the glove talons first (left).

FLYING FREE
A Eurasian eagle owl, wearing telemetry and flying jesses, flying free to its handler during training.

Above: FOOD REWARD
A free-flying Eurasian eagle owl lands on its handler's glove and has its food reward.

Additional features

Owls also have an efficient system of sensory organs that facilitate their head movements. Their large eyes are fixed in their sockets, requiring them to move their heads instead of their eyes to change their field of vision. This necessity has driven the evolution of their extraordinary head-turning ability.

Picking up your owl and initial training

When you go to the breeder to pick up your owlet, it will be covered in soft down and will be sitting quite flat-footed on the floor and will not be strong at perching. Take a nice, flat-bottomed container, such as a cat carrier or box, and line it with a towel so that the owlet can grip on to something and better stabilize itself on the journey home.

Take the owlet home and make sure you put the bird in a safe, quiet part of the house where it won't be disturbed or alarmed. No breeder should sell you an owlet that is so young that it still requires heat to survive; however, some days and nights can be cooler than average so make sure you have a heat source like a hot water bottle or heat lamp for your owlet to keep the bird nice and warm if need be.

Your owl will need feeding several times throughout the day – but do not overfeed your owlet as this can kill them. We usually feed our owlets between three and five times per day depending on the species. The rule of thumb is: an owlet will call out to you with a very harsh sound if it is hungry, so you can feed more if the young bird is giving signals to you that it's hungry.

When you are feeding the owlet, feel between the bird's legs and if the belly is firm, stop feeding it – the owlet is full. If its belly is still soft, you can give the bird more food until you feel that the belly is firm.

The owlet will grow rapidly and you can start to lessen the feeds as the bird grows into a juvenile, as it will not require as much food to grow. When the owl has grown its adult feathers and has lost all of its baby fluff, it is ready for flight training.

OWL TRAINING

All photographs: FITTING MEWS JESSES TO YOUR OWL
1. With your owl on the glove, currently wearing no equipment but anklets, take your bird's new mews jesses.

2. This will be threaded through the eyelet of the anklets so that the top button of the mews jess will fall on the outer side of the anklet, to prevent rubbing against the bird's leg.

3. Pull the jess through the eyelet.

4. Keep pulling until the jess button rests on the eyelet.

5. With one jess on, you can now put the jess in safety position.

6. Repeat this whole process with other jess, then place the owl in safety position on the glove.

179

OWL TRAINING

SAFETY POSITION
A Eurasian eagle owl rests on the glove in safety position, wearing both mews jesses and braided flying jesses.

OWL TRAINING

Owls: free flight training

It is essential that you do not tether a young owl. In the UK, it is illegal to permanently tether owls (apart from eagle owls), and I must say owls absolutely hate being tethered for long periods of time. When an owlet still has its soft, baby down feathers, its bones are extremely soft and malleable, so any form of tethering will lead to pain and deformities in its legs as it grows up. Never tether an owl until it is hard penned and of adult age.

Fit the anklets and flying jesses to your owl when it has started to flap around and is at the 'branching' stage of its life; this is when they won't sit still and are looking to fly on to every high surface they can see. It is at this point that they are becoming more independent and, if you have not done so already, you should be moving

All photographs:
ATTACHING THE SWIVEL TO THE MEWS JESSES
1. A swivel will need to be attached to the mews jesses.

2. To do this, first pass the jess through the D of the swivel.

3. Move the swivel up the jess.

4. Pass the swivel through the slit of the mews jess.

181

OWL TRAINING

5. Carefully locate the attached jess's anklet.

6. Remove the flying jess.

7. Take the second, unattached mews jess.

8. Move the jess around the back of the owl.

your owl into its enclosure, as the young owl will be fully insulated by its adult feathers and can therefore withstand any sudden drops or rises in temperature.

Your owl is now free-lofted in their enclosure and can begin to be called to your glove for free flight training. Every morning, call your bird to the glove, take up the flying jesses in your hand and weigh the owl.

Flying weight

As with the other birds that we have mentioned, the most important thing now is to work out your owl's flying weight, so monitor at which weights the bird is most responsive flying to your glove within its enclosure and take these weights as a starting point for what you would like your owl to weigh when you start the outside

9. Bring it down to join the first jess with the swivel attached, and place both jesses and the swivel into safety position.

OWL TRAINING

FITTED MEWS JESSES
A Eurasian eagle owl with both mews jesses joined together by the swivel, being held in safety position on the glove.

OWL TRAINING

All photographs: FITTING THE LEASH TO YOUR OWL
1. As with the first jess, the second will need to be attached to the swivel.

2. Pull the jess through the D of the swivel.

3. Pass the swivel through the slit of the mews jess.

4. Thread the leash through the swivel ring.

5. Keep pulling the leash through the swivel ring until the knot of the leash rests on the ring.

flying training. Write down your owl's behaviour and responsiveness to each weight so that you can start to get an idea about the weights that are working for your bird.

After weighing your owl, let it go free in its enclosure and start to jump the owl to your gloved hand for food, which is the first part of its recall training. Cut the large bits of food that you have been feeding the bird into lots of smaller bits so that the owl is still eating the same amount but is having to fly to your glove multiple times to get it. Only fly and feed your owl on the glove. Do not feed the owl if it lands on any part of your body! You need to teach the young owl that the glove is its feeding perch, and this will help negate any bad behaviour or food aggression as the owl reaches adulthood.

OWL TRAINING

A huge difference between owls and any other species of raptor is that they do not have a crop to store their food in. Most species of raptor hold their food in their crop just like chickens do, and then they digest the food over a long period of time. This means that although you have fed, for example, a Harris's hawk most of their food requirements for the day, the bird itself will still feel keen to fly because the food has not hit the bird's stomach yet. You do not get this grace period with owls. Their food will be digested immediately and will hit their stomach very soon after it goes into their beak. You can therefore overfeed your owl very easily and then you run the risk of losing your owl, as it would not be motivated to return to you for food.

Small portions

Owls are not usually very intelligent. If their bellies are full they will not think about returning to you for safety or shelter and they run an extreme risk of being predated or starving if they fly away.

With this in mind, try to cut their food up into very small pieces and never feed large amounts of food to your owl while you are out flying it – save the big rewards for when the owl is back on your glove and safely secured.

You can get a good idea about how much you can feed your owl when you are flying it to your glove in the aviary – you will soon notice that the owl is starting to slow down on the recall and to lose interest. Make a note of how much food you have given the owl and do not go over this when you are free flying the bird.

6. When the leash is correctly positioned on the swivel, you can now tie the bird to your glove using the falconer's knot.

7. Thread the leash through your glove's D-ring.

8. Tie your falconer's knot.

185

OWL TRAINING

9. Pass the tail through the loop of your falconer's knot.

10. Pull the end through to form your locking knot.

After a few days of successfully flying the owl to your glove in the aviary, it is time to attach the creance to your owl and take it to a safe area where you will teach it to fly to your glove and continue the same training outside. You can now put the mews jesses, swivel and leash on the owl in its aviary. Mark down the bird's weight and how much food you are going to feed it that day.

When you are in your outside training area, take off the leash and fit the creance to where the leash was. It is very important to secure the other end of the creance to either a post or yourself, or have a friend go with you so that they can hold on to the handle of the creance and keep control of the bird, just in case it decides to bolt during the training session.

Testing

When you are ready and have your owl in position, try to get it to jump just a few inches to your glove over the first few training sessions, using smaller bits of food that make up its total meal for the day. If the bird does not respond and is too distracted by everything around it, do not feed the bird that day; pick the owl up, reattach the mews jesses, swivel and leash and then take the bird home. Free-loft the owl back into its aviary and from now on, your owl won't get fed until it is jumping to your glove outside.

The next morning, take a note of your owl's weight (it will be lower if it didn't eat the previous day) and then see how the owl reacts out in the field at a lower weight. Mark the weight at which the bird is jumping to you now as a potential flying weight and then repeat this process

11. Your owl is now securely in position, ready for you to weigh.

until the owl is flying the full length of the creance to your gloved hand.

Over the next few days, repeat this process. When the owl is consistently flying at the same weight on the creance, you have worked out how much food you need to give it to maintain that weight, and when you are happy that the bird is responsive to your glove, you can let the owl fly free.

Before you fly your owl free, weigh the bird and make sure you are happy that it's at a weight where it has been very responsive.

Attach the telemetry equipment to your owl and make sure that you have full battery power in both the transmitter and receiver, whether you are using

OWL TRAINING

12. With your owl on your scales, weigh it – ensure you keep the leash, jesses and swivel held up to get a more accurate reading.

GPS or radio telemetry. Check the telemetry is working and on the right channels before you let the bird go. Remember: telemetry is the only way you can guarantee that you will find your bird if it gets lost – never fly any bird without telemetry.

Place the bird on the same perch in its familiar outside training area. Show your owl a nice food reward on your glove and ask the owl to jump to your glove over a small distance – a few inches is absolutely fine at this stage. If the owl is happy to jump a few inches, place it back on to its original perch and then take a step back from your original location so that you're asking the bird to jump longer and longer distances. Keep the initial free flying session very short and always reward your owl on the final flight with a large piece of food; put the jesses, swivel and leash back on the owl while it is feeding on your glove and then return it to the aviary to be free-lofted with a nice full belly of food. Your owl is now flying free and will really start to build up its muscle tone. You can start walking away from your owl in the coming weeks to encourage it to fly longer and longer distances.

Imprinted birds

Imprinted birds can be very tricky as they tend to be flown at much higher weights than parent-reared birds; they do not require being at a lower weight because you do not need to do the extensive manning process to tame your owl at the start of the training. Be careful that you do not overfeed your owl when it is out flying – they can give the impression that they are hungry but are, in fact, just calling out to you as they perceive you as their parent, and then you run the risk of the owl becoming completely unresponsive to you halfway through its flight and possibly not returning to you at all. So, keep an eye on their flying weight and do not ever fly your owl if it is very much over that weight.

HOUSING FOR BIRDS OF PREY

AVIARIES, CAGES, FURNISHINGS

HOUSING FOR BIRDS OF PREY

It is always a good idea to allow as large an enclosure as possible for your bird so that it can exercise itself by flying and jumping around the aviary, should there be a day when you can't free fly the bird yourself. There are different laws with regards to enclosure size depending on where you live in the world, but the general rule of thumb is that for your bird to act out its natural abilities and have plenty of room to fly around and explore its surroundings, the aviary must be at least three times the length of the wingspan in width, length and height. Use this as a minimum measurement and aim to go larger.

Most aviaries are made of a wooden frame and sealed with strong wood panels that are then clad with timber on the outside to make it all look prettier. You can build your aviary from bricks or a metal framework, too – it does not really matter as long as the enclosure is large enough to house the species of bird that you have chosen and it is strong enough to withstand the elements.

I always recommend that you put a concrete foundation under an aviary. Not only will this make the whole structure stronger and last you a lifetime, but it means that ground predators and rats will find it harder to burrow in and potentially kill your bird. Remember that the raw meat you feed to your bird will be very attractive to other predators, so your first thought when designing your aviary should be how to keep predators out.

Double-door system
It is advisable to have a double-door system on the entrance to your aviary, too, so that if for whatever reason your bird slips your glove or flies towards you eagerly and you are slow to close the entrance door, it can't escape out of the aviary unexpectedly.

Try to waterproof the insides of your aviary as much as possible; we have put up corrugated metal sheets around the inside of all of our aviaries so that when it comes to cleaning the birds, we only have to hose

Left: BACK GARDEN AVIARY
Your bird of prey enclosure should be large enough for free flight and should be as light and airy as possible to help maintain good health in your bird. In countries that have annual breakouts of bird flu, you must fully enclose the roof and add more windows to encourage air flow.

down and scrub the mutes (faeces) for it to disappear completely. If you leave the inside walls as bare wood, you will almost definitely get staining from the bird's mutes, which looks disgusting and, worse, can harbour bacteria because you won't be able to clean the walls properly.

The best substrate to put on the ground of your aviary is pea shingle; this material is easy to hose down and clean, and then you can rake over the cleaned shingle to level out the floor and keep the area free from mutes. It's very easy to see any uneaten food on the pea shingle, which you can take out and throw away, and you can spray a good, bird-safe disinfectant on the stones to keep it sanitized and disease-free.

Please do not use sand in any circumstances – you cannot clean this sort of substrate properly and it will harbour bacteria from any food that drops on to it and this will attract flies and therefore maggots, which are really unhealthy for your bird to be exposed to. Sand also causes impaction in the bird's crop if it takes in food that has inadvertently rolled in the sand and I have seen so many awful skin conditions as a result of sand causing abrasions under a bird's anklet or between the toes.

Above: DOUBLE-DOOR SYSTEM
A double-door system on the aviary will help to minimize the risk of your bird escaping when you are cleaning the enclosure.

Opposite: PEST DAMAGE
Rodents, foxes and other predators will be very interested in your enclosure, as the meat you feed to the bird will attract them in. Reinforce the foundations with concrete or wire mesh to prevent predators from digging into your enclosure and harming your bird.

Overleaf: FREE FLIGHT AVIARY
A free flight aviary with a covered section for the bird to shelter within during extreme heat or rain. Your enclosure must be at least three times the length of the bird's wingspan in all directions.

Roofing

You can either cover the entire enclosure with a roof or you can lay the roof over two-thirds of the enclosure so that there is a panel of open mesh at the top, which will allow more light and the weather to reach your bird. In countries where bird flu is now a problem, however, I would recommend that you cover the whole aviary

HOUSING FOR BIRDS OF PREY

to stop any wild birds from defecating into your bird's enclosure and potentially spreading the disease to your bird. We have done this for our enclosures and, to let more light in, we have used transparent skylight sheeting, which we have fitted in panels across the roof – this works brilliantly to let natural light flood the aviary without risking the health of the birds that are housed safely inside.

Think about the area where you are going to build your aviary, too; if there is very little sunshine in that place all day, then it might be nice to put more skylights in the roof if you're going for a fully covered enclosure, or perhaps an extra window so that you are maximizing the amount of light that can reach your bird in its enclosure. If you are planning on building the aviary in an area with lots of direct sun, try to think about shaded areas within the aviary so that your bird can find some cooler areas in the real heat of the day.

Window panels

It is always a good idea to have one or two large window panels at the front and/or side of your aviary so that your bird can look out at the world from its enclosure and get some enrichment from watching nature in action. There are several different ways to cover the window panels but the best method that we have found is a fine-gauge, soft metal material called ClearMesh, which is extremely strong, almost transparent when you paint it black, and will not allow any insects or wild birds to fly into the enclosure, which again helps prevent health problems and diseases from entering the enclosure.

Try to avoid chicken wire or galvanized mesh as this will shred the bird's feathers if it flies on to the material (which your bird absolutely will!) and with the harder, thinner metal materials, your bird can also cut its feet, which can cause serious health problems in the future.

Some people put canes or wooden barring of some description down the windows, which is great for stopping the bird grabbing at mesh and damaging its feet and feathers, but it absolutely will not stop wild birds or rats getting in, which is something to consider if you have bird flu in your country or you have a lot of rodents in your area.

HOUSING FOR BIRDS OF PREY

Furnishing

You can furnish your aviary however you like but remember: natural is normally best! Try putting in as many variable-sized branches as possible all around the aviary so that your bird has plenty of choice when it comes to seating areas. We also put in logs and large stones or rocks, which we place on the floor of our aviaries so that the birds can forage on the ground or sit lower if they choose to. Birds of prey always feel more comfortable if there is somewhere to hide, so you can plant small trees and bushes in their aviary to give them plenty of screening. It's also a great idea to wrap some artificial grass around the branches in places or secure artificial grass to some favoured flat areas where your bird likes to sit. Artificial grass can help prevent bumblefoot in birds of prey, as it offers a different texture and stops sores and calluses developing over time.

Always provide your bird with fresh water daily – you can either buy a specialized falconry bath (these come in a variety of shapes and sizes to fit any bird) or an alternative that works just as well and is far cheaper or easier to find is some plant pot trays, which hold plenty of water for a small or medium-sized bird of prey.

Sadly, your bird may well become a target for theft, so try to foresee any problems before they occur and do your best to prevent your bird from being stolen. You can put pea shingle around the outside of your aviary so that you can hear footsteps more easily and I would recommend a security light facing your aviary so that any unwanted movement will be picked up and highlighted immediately. The best thing you can do to stop a thief is to make it as hard as possible to get to your bird, so I would recommend that you lock every door and entrance securely with a padlock and chain.

However you choose to build your aviary, the most important thing is to have the enclosure built, fully furnished and ready to house your chosen species of bird before you pick it up. Make sure it is built to the correct size for your bird when it is a fully matured adult and keep the aviary clean on a daily basis to ensure good health for your bird throughout its lifetime.

Right: PERCHING MATERIALS
Secure different types of perching within the aviary to help prevent bumblefoot and sores on your bird's feet. Astroturf can be fitted to any surface and this helps relieve pressure around the bottom of your bird's feet.

TRAINING AVIARY
A fully enclosed aviary is essential in colder climates and can help prevent zoonotic diseases from entering the enclosure. Zoo mesh provides a safe window material that stops wildlife from getting into the enclosure and passing disease to your bird. It will also prevent tail and feather damage, as the feathers can't pass through the smaller holes and be stripped away by the metal.

FEEDING YOUR BIRD OF PREY

TYPES OF FOOD, PREPARATION, HYGIENE

FEEDING YOUR BIRD OF PREY

As birds of prey are carnivores, their diet has to be entirely meat-based. There are some birds of prey that can eat insects and even fruit on occasion but, in the main, their diet will consist of birds, fish and mammals, depending on the species.

It is, of course, always best to contact a reputable animal food supplier and ask what they can provide – the food you buy from these places is sanitary and bred for the purpose of feeding other animals so they are usually given a good, nutritious diet that will be better for your bird.

The most popular food to feed captive raptors is day-old chicks, which can be bought in bulk, are easy to store and are relatively cheap to buy. Birds of prey absolutely love day-old chicks, but care must be taken that you do not overfeed them too much yolk that is stored inside the chick, because this can cause high cholesterol over time. As a rule of thumb, you should feed whole, yolky chick to your bird no more than three days per week. You can de-yolk the chicks once they are thawed out to help prevent overfeeding too much fat. You can buy day-old chicks from any reputable animal food supplier, and they will usually be delivered to you frozen so that you can defrost what you need on a daily basis.

Quail is a very popular food, too, as it is far higher in nutrients than day-old chicks and most birds of prey seem to really enjoy the taste of it! Ex-egg-layer quails are cost-effective and you can even buy quails that have been enhanced with vitamins to help your bird through the moult. Again, quail can be purchased through any reputable animal food supplier and they will usually be delivered to you frozen so that you can defrost what you need on a daily basis.

Rats are extremely nutritious food for birds of prey and we tend to feed rat to any bird that we want to put weight on quickly, because it is very rich meat, so a bird will gain weight rapidly after eating rat. It is worth preparing the rat by taking out the guts, which can contain a lot of bacteria, and I would always recommend cutting the tail off and chopping it into

Right: GLOVE HYGIENE
As well as the food preparation room, your falconry glove must be kept meticulously clean. Bacteria can grow on the surface of the glove quickly, so always clean it after each training session.

FEEDING YOUR BIRD OF PREY

Above & opposite: FEEDING ON THE GLOVE
A well balanced diet is essential for any bird of prey. Make sure you feed a good variety of food, including: day old chicks, rats, mice and quail, to keep your bird happy and healthy.

smaller pieces, as there have been records of birds choking on a rat tail as it got caught in their crop and throat. Rat teeth are very sharp, so it is advisable to cut them out before feeding it to your bird to avoid any internal injuries.

Wild food

There may be times when you are offered wild animals that have been killed in the field to feed your bird. It can be a really good way of obtaining high-quality food free of charge; however, you must be very vigilant and ask how the animal was killed before you feed it to your bird.

Game birds such as pheasants, grouse, ducks and geese can be fed to your bird and are often shot. If the hunters were using lead shot, this can be lethal to your bird if it is ingested. Always make sure that you only accept animals that have been shot with steel shot or have been snared or killed without the use of lead or poisons in any way.

Roadkill can be risky, too – you do not know if the animal was in good health before being hit by a car; it could have been shot or poisoned and then wandered into the road before being put out of its misery. It is almost impossible to know how long the animal has been left in the road, too, so the meat could be starting to decompose or attract flies, which will lay eggs in the meat and cause a maggot infestation, which is really unpleasant and terrible for your bird's health. As cars pass the carcass, fumes and oil particles can fall on the body, too, so I would always recommend that if you are going to feed roadkill to your bird, you skin the whole carcass and take out the guts to minimize any kind of health risk.

If your bird catches any wild animals out in the field, it is a good idea to allow your bird to feed on the kill and then trade with the bird – give it a large piece of food on your glove so that you can prepare the carcass later and inspect the skin for any shot wounds or disease.

When your bird is moulting, you can also give them nutritional supplements in the form of powder that is sprinkled over their food, which can help their feather condition.

FEEDING YOUR BIRD OF PREY

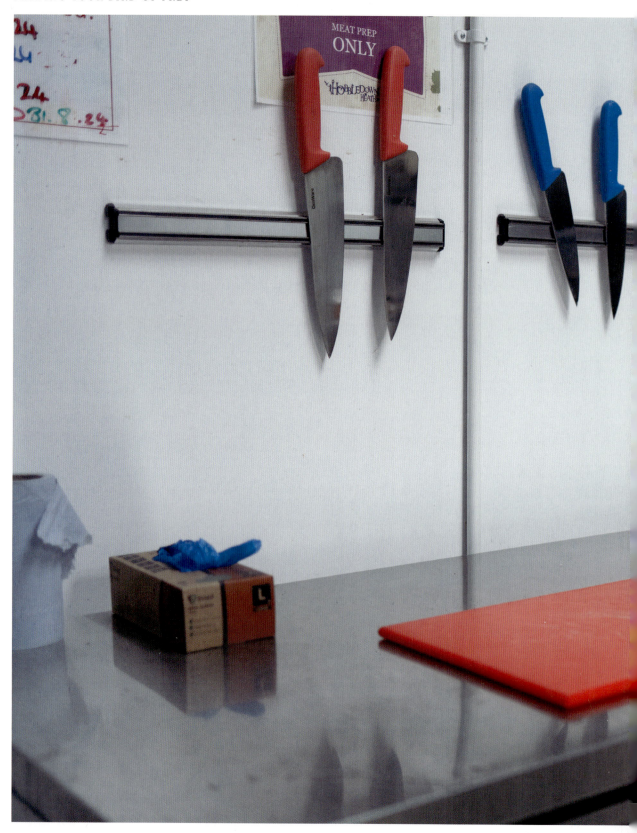

FEEDING YOUR BIRD OF PREY

KITCHEN
To avoid foreign bodies and cross-contamination, a well-organized, clean workspace that you can dedicate to your bird's food preparation is highly important.

COMMON PITFALLS

INJURIES, DISEASES, ENVIRONMENTAL FACTORS

Bumblefoot

Bumblefoot, or pododermatitis, is a common and often debilitating condition affecting the feet of captive birds of prey. It manifests as a range of symptoms, from mild redness and swelling to severe, deep-seated infections that can lead to systemic illness and even death if untreated. This condition is of particular concern in captive raptors, given their reliance on healthy feet for hunting, perching and overall well-being.

Bumblefoot is a significant health concern for captive birds of prey, necessitating diligent care and management to prevent and treat. Recognizing the symptoms early and understanding which species are most at risk can aid in implementing effective preventative measures. Through careful environmental management, proper nutrition and regular veterinary oversight, the incidence and severity of bumblefoot can be minimized, ensuring the well-being of these magnificent birds in captivity.

Symptoms of bumblefoot in captive birds of prey
Early stage (Grade I)
Mild redness and swelling: The initial signs include slight redness and swelling on the plantar surface of the foot. There may be minimal discomfort.
Lameness: The bird might show slight lameness or favour one foot over the other.

Intermediate stage (Grades II–III)
Development of lesions: The condition progresses to the formation of small, localized sores. These lesions can become infected, causing pain and discomfort.

Swelling and heat: As the infection sets in, the affected area may become swollen and warm to the touch.
Lameness: More pronounced lameness and reluctance to perch are normally evident. The bird may avoid using the affected foot altogether.
Weeping fluids: In some cases, pus or other exudate may be present, indicating a more severe infection.

Advanced stage (Grades IV–V)
Severe ulceration and necrosis: In advanced cases, the infection can cause severe ulceration and necrosis of the bodily tissues. The foot may appear blackened and necrotic.
Abscesses: Large abscesses can form, filled with pus, and potentially lead to the spread of infection to bones and joints.
Systemic illness: If the infection becomes systemic, the bird can exhibit signs of generalized illness, such as lethargy, decreased appetite and weight loss.
Severe lameness or inability to stand: The bird may be unable to stand or use the affected foot, severely impacting its quality of life.

Birds of prey most at risk
Several factors contribute to the susceptibility of certain birds of prey to bumblefoot. These factors include species-specific anatomy, captive environment conditions and individual health status.

Species susceptibility
Falcons (e.g. peregrine falcons, gyrfalcons): Falcons are particularly prone to bumblefoot due to their unique foot anatomy, which includes long, slender toes with less protective padding. The pressure points created during perching can predispose them to foot lesions.

Hawks (e.g. red-tailed hawks, Harris's hawks): These birds are also at risk, especially if they are overweight

Left & opposite: TREATING BUMBLEFOOT
A bird being put under anaesthesia in order for its bandages to be changed (left). The bandages serve to protect the bird from further infection as well as to provide some minor comfort. Bumblefoot is not only painful for birds, but can be an easily avoidable, life-threatening condition (right).

or if their perches are inappropriate. Hawks have relatively larger feet than falcons, which can spread out the pressure, but improper perching still poses a significant risk.

Opposite: RED-TAILED HAWK
Captive birds will often have overgrown beaks due to their continuous, nutritious diet and lack of solid bones to wear their beaks down naturally. The falconer must be prepared to file or 'cope' the bird's beak when it becomes too long, as an overgrown beak can affect the bird's ability to eat.

Below: INJURIES
Other potential injuries found in birds of prey include wing and leg breaks due to impact damage while they are hunting. Here a raptor education group handles a bald eagle with a wing injury in the organization's clinic.

Eagles (e.g. bald eagles, golden eagles): Eagles have large, powerful feet and talons that can be prone to bumblefoot, especially in captivity, where they may be less active and more prone to weight gain and poor foot health.

Owls (e.g. great horned owls, barn owls): Owls, with their broad, heavily feathered feet, can also suffer from bumblefoot, particularly if they are kept in enclosures with unsuitable substrates that do not mimic their natural perching environments.

Environmental factors
Perching surfaces: Captive birds often perch on artificial surfaces that do not mimic the natural branches they would use in the wild. Hard, smooth or abrasive perches can cause repetitive stress injuries to the feet.

COMMON PITFALLS

Hygiene: Poor hygiene in enclosures can lead to the build-up of bacteria and other pathogens, increasing the risk of infection if the skin is broken.
Diet: Nutritional deficiencies, particularly in vitamins A and E, can affect skin health and the bird's ability to heal from minor injuries.

Individual health factors
Obesity: Overweight birds place more pressure on their feet, which can exacerbate or predispose them to developing bumblefoot.
Inactivity: Captive birds often lack the exercise they would naturally get in the wild, leading to poorer circulation and increased susceptibility to foot problems.
Age: Older birds are more prone to bumblefoot due to age-related changes in skin elasticity and general health.

Prevention and management
Preventing bumblefoot in captive birds of prey involves a multifaceted approach:
Perch design: Provide natural, variable perching options that mimic the bird's natural environment and

Above: BUMBLEFOOT
It's important that your bird's perches are appropriate and maintained well, as an inappropriate surface, as well as poor hygiene, increase the risk of your bird suffering from bumblefoot.

Opposite: UNDERSTANDING YOUR BIRD
Getting to know your bird's habits and behaviours means you will quickly notice changes in its health, as a normally alert, responsive bird can become irritable or withdrawn.

help distribute pressure more evenly and reduce the risk of injury.
Hygiene: Maintain clean enclosures and perches to minimize the risk of infection.
Diet and weight management: Ensure a balanced diet and maintain an appropriate weight to reduce pressure on the feet.
Regular veterinary care: Routine health checks by a veterinarian specializing in avian medicine can help detect and treat early signs of bumblefoot.

Aspergillus

Aspergillus is a genus of fungi known to cause aspergillosis, a serious respiratory disease in birds,

including birds of prey. This condition is particularly problematic in captive settings due to the increased exposure to fungal spores and stress-related factors that can compromise birds' immune systems. Understanding the symptoms and risk factors, and identifying the most at-risk species, is essential for early diagnosis and effective management, ultimately ensuring the health and well-being of these birds.

Symptoms of aspergillosis in birds of prey

The signs of aspergillosis in birds of prey vary and are largely dependent on the severity and location of the infection. The disease manifests primarily in two forms: acute and chronic.

Acute aspergillosis: This form is often rapidly fatal and occurs when a bird inhales a large number of spores. Symptoms can appear suddenly and include:
- Respiratory distress: Rapid breathing, open-mouthed breathing and increased respiratory effort.
- Lethargy: Affected birds may appear unusually tired, weak and less responsive.
- Loss of appetite: Birds may refuse to eat, leading to rapid weight loss.
- Voice changes: Hoarseness or loss of voice due to inflammation of the syrinx.
- Sudden death: In some cases, birds may die without showing significant prior symptoms.

Chronic aspergillosis: This form develops more

slowly and can be challenging to diagnose early. Symptoms include:

- Respiratory issues: Chronic respiratory signs such as coughing, wheezing and nasal discharge.
- Weight loss: Progressive weight loss despite a good appetite.
- Poor feather condition: Birds may have ruffled or unkempt feathers.
- Behavioural changes: Reduced activity levels and decreased interest in usual activities.
- Swelling: Visible swelling around the face or neck if the infection spreads to air sacs or sinuses.
- Neurological signs: If the fungus invades the central nervous system, symptoms like incoordination and seizures may occur.

Diagnosing aspergillosis often requires a combination of clinical signs, imaging (such as X-rays or CT scans), endoscopy and laboratory tests, including fungal cultures and serology. Early detection is crucial for effective treatment, which typically involves antifungal medications, supportive care and environmental management to reduce spore exposure.

Birds of prey most at risk

Certain species of birds of prey are more susceptible to aspergillosis due to their natural history, captive management practices and inherent physiological differences. The following birds of prey are considered most at risk:

Gyrfalcon (*Falco rusticolus*): Known for their high susceptibility to aspergillosis, especially in captivity. Their natural Arctic habitat has low fungal spore counts, making them less adapted to environments with higher fungal loads.

Peregrine falcon (*Falco peregrinus*): Although hardy in the wild, captive peregrine falcons can develop aspergillosis due to stress and confinement.

Red-tailed hawk (*Buteo jamaicensis*): Commonly kept in captivity, these birds are prone to respiratory infections, including aspergillosis, particularly when stressed or exposed to poor air quality.

Snowy owl (*Bubo scandiacus*): Like gyrfalcons, snowy owls originate from Arctic regions with minimal fungal exposure, making them vulnerable to aspergillosis in captivity.

Northern goshawk (*Accipiter gentilis*): These birds

Opposite: GYRFALCON BLENDS IN
Like the snowy owl, gyrfalcons normally reside in the tundra, so are susceptible to aspergillosis and bumblefoot when in captivity.

are highly sensitive to stress and poor husbandry conditions, increasing their risk of aspergillosis.

Golden eagle (*Aquila chrysaetos*): Larger birds like golden eagles have a substantial respiratory system, making them more prone to inhaling large quantities of fungal spores.

The susceptibility of these species can be attributed to several factors:

- Environmental stress: Captivity inherently imposes stress due to confinement, handling and close proximity to humans. Stress suppresses the immune system, making birds more vulnerable to infections.
- Air quality: Poor ventilation and high humidity in aviaries can promote fungal growth. Birds housed in such conditions are at higher risk of inhaling *Aspergillus* spores.
- Diet and nutrition: Inadequate nutrition can weaken a bird's immune response. Birds of prey require specific diets rich in essential nutrients, and any deficiencies can predispose them to infections.
- Natural habitat differences: Birds from colder, arid climates with low fungal spore counts, such as gyrfalcons and snowy owls, are less adapted to environments with higher fungal loads.

Prevention and management

Preventing aspergillosis involves meticulous husbandry practices:

- Environmental control: Ensuring good ventilation, reducing humidity and maintaining cleanliness in aviaries can greatly minimize fungal spore levels.
- Stress reduction: Minimizing handling and disturbances, providing enrichment and ensuring appropriate social interactions can reduce stress.
- Nutritional support: Providing a balanced diet tailored to the species' needs helps maintain a robust immune system.
- Regular health monitoring: Routine health checks and early intervention at the first sign of illness are crucial.

COMMON PITFALLS

COMMON PITFALLS

Overgrown beak and talons

Due to the highly nutritious food that captive birds of prey get on a daily basis, the beak and talons can overgrow fairly quickly. In the wild, where the birds are always at a nutritional deficit, their beak and talons rarely get overgrown, as they simply have not got the extra nutrients to grow them extensively.

You can put hard, natural perching into your aviary to help to wear down your bird's talons. To wear the beak down naturally, you can also introduce food like rabbit heads or large, whole body portions of food, as the beak will naturally wear down on the strong bone.

If your bird still has an overgrown beak and talons, you will need to cope (file) the beak and trim the talons with animal nail clippers to stop them from getting too long and interfering with feeding or perching. Remember, the number one reason for bumblefoot is overgrown talons: they can puncture the soft pad of the foot and then infection can get in and spread quickly, so always maintain good foot and beak health so that your bird can remain healthy and happy.

Below: GOLDEN EAGLE
In the wild, the golden eagle will keep its continually growing beak in shape by 'feaking' – rubbing its beak against hard surfaces such as rocks or trees. Always maintain good ventilation and plenty of windows in a captive bird's aviary to lessen the likelihood of disease.

PUBLIC PERCEPTION

In modern times and with so much negativity being spread about captive animals on social media platforms, there has never been a greater need for good falconry practices to make sure that we are educating the world on how important it is to maintain a captive population of raptors.

Not only do captive birds of prey help directly to stabilize and increase wild populations of their species in the form of conservation breeding projects, but they also help increase our knowledge of medical requirements needed to rehabilitate wild, injured raptors. By working with veterinary teams across the world, falconers have enabled vets to make huge breakthroughs in repairing broken bones, immunization against diseases and identifying environmental factors that can affect breeding and hunting conditions. By collating this data and using it out in the field, falconry has helped save a number of critically endangered raptors. This means that the biodiversity can be increased and the natural ecosystem can be restored to a healthy, successful territory that future generations can enjoy.

Never underestimate how important it is to spread this positive message of conservation and welfare to people who may not understand the important work that ambassador animals do for their wild counterparts – when you own a bird of prey, you are responsible not only for that bird, but also for the reputation of all falconers and conservationists who are working hard to make sure the world has a healthy population of raptors in the wild.

Always make sure you step out with education in mind and be polite to people who want to know more about the bird you are flying; trust me, when you fly a bird free out where the public can see them, you will become a beacon to everyone, as it is such a special and unusual thing for people to see! By being respectful and kind, you help to put a positive message out there that people who keep birds of prey in captivity are approachable and are doing a great job not just for their bird, but for the environment too.

Enjoy your new partnership with your feathered friend and share your stories about your training with others. It really is a unique and special experience having a bond with a bird of prey. They will teach you so much about humility, nature and the freedom of the air – when they return to you after each flight, you will have an enormous sense of accomplishment which you absolutely deserve to feel after putting in so much work to tame an ancient predator of the sky. Falconry has survived for thousands of years and with each new person introduced to the sport, it will secure its place in human history for many thousands of years to come.

APPENDICES

Avian veterinary services

The importance of specialized veterinary care for birds of prey cannot be overstated. These amazing creatures possess unique physiological and behavioural characteristics that necessitate specialized knowledge and treatment approaches that go beyond the capabilities of general veterinary practice. Ensuring their health and wellbeing requires a deep understanding of their anatomy, diet, behaviours and the specific ailments they are prone to.

Moreover, their contributions to conservation, research and education help ensure that raptors continue to thrive in both wild and captive environments. As representatives of these majestic creatures, it is our responsibility to provide them with the highest standard of care through the services of specialized veterinary professionals.

Understanding Specialized Anatomy and Physiology
Birds of prey have unique anatomical and physiological features that differentiate them from other bird species. Their powerful talons, sharp beaks, keen eyesight and specialized flight muscles all require expert attention. Specialized veterinarians, often called avian or raptor veterinarians, have extensive training in these areas. They are adept at diagnosing issues related to these specialized structures, such as fractures or infections in talons and beaks, which general veterinarians might not be familiar with.

Disease Recognition and Treatment
Raptors are susceptible to various diseases and parasites, some of which are specific to their species. Conditions such as aspergillosis (a fungal infection), bumblefoot (a bacterial infection of the foot) and West Nile virus are examples of ailments that can affect these birds. Avian-specific veterinary care is absolutely necessary for early recognition

and relevant treatment of these conditions. Veterinarians with experience in avian medicine can identify subtle signs of illness that might be missed by those less familiar with these species, leading to more effective and timely interventions.

Nutrition and Dietary Needs
The dietary requirements of birds of prey are significantly different from those of other birds. Raptors are carnivorous and require a diet rich in protein and specific nutrients found in their prey. Specialized veterinarians can provide guidance on proper nutrition, ensuring that birds receive the necessary vitamins and minerals to maintain their health. They can also diagnose and treat nutritional deficiencies or imbalances, which can lead to severe health problems if not addressed.

Rehabilitative Care
Birds of prey often suffer injuries in the wild, such as fractures from collisions or gunshot wounds. Specialized veterinary care is crucial for the rehabilitation of these injured birds. Avian veterinarians have the skills to perform delicate surgeries and provide post-operative care tailored to the needs of raptors. Their expertise in creating and managing rehabilitation programmes is vital for the successful release of these birds back into the wild.

Behavioural Understanding
Raptors exhibit unique behaviours that require specialized knowledge to interpret and manage. Understanding these behaviours is essential for both the medical and psychological wellbeing of the birds. Specialized veterinarians are trained to recognize signs of stress, aggression or other behavioural issues and can advise on appropriate environmental enrichments and handling techniques to mitigate these problems.

Preventative Care and Husbandry
Preventative care is an essential part of maintaining the health of birds of prey. Regular check-ups with a specialized veterinarian can help catch potential health issues before they become serious. Avian veterinarians can provide advice on proper husbandry practices, such as housing, sanitation and preventative measures against common diseases. This proactive approach helps ensure that raptors live long, healthy lives, whether they are in captivity or part of conservation programmes.

Conservation Efforts
Birds of prey often play a significant role in conservation efforts due to their position at the top of the food chain and their sensitivity to environmental changes. Specialized veterinary care is essential for the success of breeding and reintroduction programmes aimed at preserving endangered raptor species. Veterinarians with expertise in avian medicine contribute to these efforts by ensuring that the health and genetic diversity of breeding populations are maintained, as well as by treating and rehabilitating injured birds that can contribute to these populations.

Research and Education
Specialized veterinary care for birds of prey also supports ongoing research and education. Avian veterinarians often collaborate with researchers to study diseases, behaviours and ecology of raptors. This research has the potential to result in improved conservation strategies and medical treatments. Moreover, these veterinarians play a crucial role in educating the public and other veterinarians about the unique needs and challenges of caring for birds of prey, fostering a broader understanding and appreciation of these remarkable animals.

Glossary

Accipiter: Genus of raptor, short-winged hawks; e.g. goshawks. Austringer: One who hunts with hawks.
Bal-chatri: A cage-like trap with live bait and monofilament nooses that catch the raptor by the feet.
Bate: An attempt to fly either on the fist or perch when secured; usually a few flaps.

Bind: To grab and hold quarry.
Brancher: A young hawk, mostly feathered but not yet fully capable of flight.
Buteo: Genus of raptor, broad-winged hawks; e.g. the red-tailed hawk.
Cadge: A portable perch capable of holding several birds.
Cast: The regurgitation of

indigestible parts of quarry (fur and bones), a normal daily act; or two raptors flown together; or to physically hold a raptor to prevent movement.
Casting: The act of catching and securing a bird of prey in your grasp that minimizes damage and unnecessary anxiety to the bird. Also used to refer to

the pellet cast by a bird of prey.
Coping: The act of filing back a bird's beak.
Creance: Long training cord or leash.
Crepuscular: Hunts during dusk and/or dawn.
Crop: Muscular, expandable pouch where excess food is stored to digest later.

220

Diurnal: Hunts during daytime.

Enter: When a trained raptor first captures a type of quarry.

Eyass: A young raptor before fledging.

Eyrie: A raptor nest site.

Feak: When the bird cleans its beak.

Flush: The use of dogs to cause the quarry to flee from its cover.

Hack: Leaving a bird free for a time to develop flying skills.

Haggard: A raptor more than a year old.

Hard penned: Fully grown feathers.

Imping: A method of repairing broken feathers.

Imprint: When a bird of prey is raised by someone other than their parent. The human will act as their parent and so the bird will call to humans for food.

Intermewed: A raptor that has moulted in captivity.

Jesses: The leather straps used to hold the bird of prey while it is on the fist. These can be found with small slits at the end to attach a swivel or without, for when they're flying free.

Lure: A small, usually horseshoe-shaped object at the end of a thin rope used by the falconer to replicate a bird in flight for falcons to catch. Sometimes decorated by the falconer in the feathers of the prey they would like their bird to catch, such as crow, pigeon or magpie. There is also a rabbit lure that serves a similar purpose and is used with some birds of prey that catch rabbits, such as hawks.

Manning: Spending time with a bird of prey so they get used to your presence and company, therefore gaining confidence and trust.

Mantle: To hide food from onlookers by surrounding it with their wings.

Mews: Housing for raptors.

Mutes: Faecal matter.

Nocturnal: Hunts during the night time.

Pass: Where a bird of prey stoops for a lure and passes it without catching it. Also used to refer to the mating process where the male presents and passes food to the female in an attempt to mate.

Passager: A raptor within the first year of its life.

Pellet: A small ball 'thrown up' by birds of prey containing the indigestible parts of their prey such as bones, feathers, fur etc.

Pitch: Height a falcon takes overhead, usually expressed in feet.

Preen: Straightening feathers with the beak, grooming.

Quarry: Specifically, game hunted by hawks. Also, one that is sought or pursued.

Rouse: Shaking feathers out as a grooming action; when a bird of prey lifts all of the feathers on its body and shakes. They do this for a number of reasons, such as to trap heat, realign their feathers and shake off any debris and downy feathers.

Slip: To release the raptor to chase after quarry.

Soar: When a bird of prey 'catches' a thermal and rests in it high in the sky, where they are then able to rest in between wing beats.

Stoop: Rapid descent from altitude, usually when in pursuit of quarry. The bird of prey folds its wings into its body, which makes them more aerodynamic so they can move through the air much faster to catch their prey.

Swivel: A metal object used to secure a bird's jesses that turns and spins to prevent tangling.

Telemetry: Electronic gear for tracking lost raptors.

Tiercel: A male falcon.

Tiring: Tough piece of meat to pull and eat tediously.

Wait on: The falcon maintaining pitch over the falconer.

Warble: An overhead wing stretch.

Weather: To put a bird outside to enjoy the weather; secured.

Yarak: State of mind in accipiters and hawks eager to hunt.

Useful links

BIRD OF PREY WEBCAMS

Nottinghamshire Wildlife Trust, Peregrine Falcon Live Nest Cam: https://www.nottinghamshirewildlife.org/peregrine-cam

NTU Falcon Cam Facebook group: https://www.facebook.com/groups/nottinghamtufalconcam

Leicester Peregrines: http://leicesterperegrines.org.uk

Derby Peregrines: https://derbyperegrines.blogspot.com/p/our-webcams.html

Hawk Watch: https://hawkwatch.org

Sheffield Peregrines: http://peregrine.group.shef.ac.uk

Sussex Wildlife Trust, Kestrel Cam: https://sussexwildlifetrust.org.uk/kestrelcam

Sea-EagleCAM Live Video: https://www.sea-eaglecam.org/video.html

Delaware Ornithological Society: https://www.dosbirds.org/citizen-science/falcon-watch

UK FALCONRY SERVICES

Independent Bird Register: http://www.independentbirdregister.co.uk

NatureScot / NàdarAlba: https://www.nature.scot

US FALCONRY ORGANIZATIONS

North American Falconers Association: https://www.n-a-f-a.com

American Falconry Conservation: http://www.falconryconservancy.org

United States Fish and Wildlife:https://www.fws.gov

INTERNATIONAL FALCONRY ORGANIZATIONS

International Association for Falconry and Conservation of Birds of Prey: https://iaf.org

Falconry Heritage Trust: https://falconryheritage.org

UK NATIONAL CLUBS

British Falconers' Club: https://www.britishfalconersclub.co.uk/New_Site

Scottish Hawking Club: http://www.scottishhawkingclub.co.uk

Welsh Hawking Club: https://welshhawkingclub.org

Irish Hawking Club: http://www.irishhawkingclub.ie

UK REGIONAL CLUBS

Cheshire and North Wales Hawking Club: https://www.facebook.com/groups/1211552709807540

Home Counties Falconry Club: http://homecountieshawkingclub.org.uk

Northern England Falconry Club: https://www.northernenglandfalconryclub.co.uk

South East Falconry Group: https://sefg.org.uk

South East Raptors Association: http://www.seraonline.org.uk

Tees Valley Hawking Club: https://en-gb.facebook.com/teesvalleyhawkingclub

Yorkshire Falconry Club: https://yorkshirefalconryclub.co.uk

APPENDICES

US STATE CLUBS

Alabama: https://www.alabamafalconry.com

Alaska: https://akfalconers.com

Arizona: https://arizonafalconers.com

Arkansas: https://arkansashawkingassociation.org

California: http://www.calhawkingclub.org

Colorado: https://www.coloradohawkingclub.com

Connecticut: https://ctfalconers.wixsite.com/home

Florida Falconers' Association: https://www.floridafalconry.com

Georgia Game Hawkers Club: https://www.georgiagamehawkers.com

Georgia Falconry Association: https://gafalconryassociation167829130.wordpress.com

Idaho: https://www.idahofalconers.org

Great Lakes Falconers' Association (Illinois): https://greatlakesfalconers.org

Indiana Falconers Association: http://www.indianafalconersassociation.org

Iowa Falconer: https://iowafalconer.com

Kansas Hawking Club: https://www.kansashawkingclub.org

Kentucky Falconers Association: https://www.kentuckyfalconry.com

Louisiana Wildlife & Fisheries: https://www.wlf.louisiana.gov/page/falconry

Maine Falconry & Raptor Conservancy: https://www.mainefalconers.org

Maryland Department of Natural Resources: https://dnr.maryland.gov/wildlife/Pages/Licenses/falconry.aspx

Massachusetts Falconry and Hawk Trust: https://massachusettsfalconryandhawktrust.wordpress.com

Michigan Hawking Club: https://mhc.clubexpress.com

Minnesota Falconers Association: http://www.mnfalconry.org

Mississippi Wildlife & Fisheries Falconry Program: https://www.mdwfp.com/wildlife-hunting/wildlife-species-program/falconry-program

Missouri Falconer's Association: https://missourifalconersassociation.com

Montana Falconers Association: http://montanafalconers.org

Nebraska Game Parks: https://outdoornebraska.gov/hunt/prepare-to-hunt/falconry

Nevada Falconry: https://www.nevadafalconry.com

New Jersey Falconry Club: https://www.newjerseyfalconryclub.com

New Mexico Falconers' Association: https://www.nmfalconry.com/about-falconry

New York State Falconry Association: https://nysfa.org

North Carolina Falconer's Guild: https://northcarolinafalconersguild.org

North Dakota Game and Fish: https://gf.nd.gov/hunting/falconry

Ohio Falconry Association: https://www.ohiofalconry.org

Oklahoma Falconers Association: https://www.okfalconersassoc.com

Oregon Falconers Association: https://oregonfalconers.com

Pennsylvania Falconry & Hawk Trust: https://pafalconryandhawktrust.com

South Carolina Falconry Association: https://www.southcarolinafalconryassociation.com

South Dakota Game, Fish & Parks: https://gfp.sd.gov/falconry-permit

Tennessee Wildlife Resources Agency: https://www.tn.gov/twra/law-enforcement/permits/falconry.html

Texas Hawking Association: https://www.texashawking.org

Utah Falconers Association: https://www.utahfalconers.com

Virginia Falconers' Association: http://www.vafalconers.com

Washington Falconer's Association: https://wafalconersassociation.org

West Virginia Falconry Club: https://www.wvfalconry.org

Wisconsin Falconers Association: https://www.wisconsinfalconers.org

Wyoming Falconers Association: https://wyomingfalconersassociation.com

SPECIALIST VET SERVICES

Great Western Exotics: https://www.gwexotics.com/raptors-pet-owner

Avian Veterinary Services: http://avianveterinaryservices.co.uk

Association of Avian Veterinarians: https://www.aav.org

Abu Dhabi Falcon Hospital: https://www.falconhospital.com

FALCONRY FOOD SUPPLIERS

Honeybrook Animal Foods: https://www.honeybrookfoods.co.uk

Kiezebrink UK Ltd: https://www.kiezebrink.co.uk

BIRD OF PREY CHARITIES

All About Birds: https://www.allaboutbirds.org

Featherwell Foundation: https://featherwellfoundation.org

HawkWatch International: https://hawkwatch.org

Philippine Eagle Foundation: https://www.philippineeaglefoundation.org

Raptor Aid: https://www.raptoraid.com/about

Raptor Rescue: http://www.raptorrescue.org.uk

Raptor Research Foundation: https://www.raptorresearchfoundation.org

Saker Conservation and Falconry: http://www.sakerfalcon.org/1/saker-conservation-and-falconry

The Peregrine Fund: https://www.peregrinefund.org

Vulpro: https://www.vulpro.com

Index

Accipiter, definition 220
African spotted eagle-owl (*Bubo africanus*) 68
all-in-one anklet and jess 28
Ancient Greece 8, 11
anklets 24, 25–8, 29, 75
  owls 179, 181
Aplomado falcon (*Falco femoralis*) 33, 70
  see also falcons (general)
Aristotle 8, 11
Article 10 certificates 35
aspergillosis 214–18
  prevention and management 216–18
  susceptibility 216
  symptoms 215–16
aviaries 191–9
  double-door system 191
  foundations and substrate 191–2, 193
  free flight 194–5
  furnishing 196
  roofing 192–3
  security 196
  training aviary 198–9
  window panels 193

bal-chatri 220
bald eagle 27, 213
  see also eagles (general)
barn owl (*Tyto alba*) 60, 61, 71, 77
bating 36, 86, 89, 96, 220
Bayeaux Tapestry 10
beaks
  coping 33–9, 212, 218
  feaking 218, 221
binding 126, 220
bird carrier 33, 140, 178
bird flu 192–3
block perch 20, 23, 24
bow perch 20, 22–3, 23–4, 89
branching 181, 220
bumblefoot 210–14
  environmental factors 213–14
  health factors 214
  prevention and management 23–4, 196, 214
  susceptibility 210, 213–14
  symptoms 210
  treatment 210–11
buzzards (general) 43, 44, 49, 69, 82
  hunting training 159, 161

cadge 220
cast (group of hawks) 49
cast (pellets) 220
casting 36–7, 220
  casting jacket 36–7
China, falconry in 8
claw cutting 34, 35, 36–9, 218
common buzzard (*Buteo buteo*) 69, 159
conservation 35, 219
coping/coping files 33–9, 212, 218
creance 220
  attaching 120–1, 172–4, 186
  definition 32–3, 220
  lure training 126–9

owl training 172–5, 186
  recall training 120–2
crepuscular 60, 220
crop 185, 192, 205, 220

diet 202–7
diseases 220
  aspergillosis 214–18
  bumblefoot 210–14
diurnal 221
donor feathers 35, 221
double-door system 191, 192
dummy bunny 159

eagles (general) 16
  aggressiveness 82, 159
  aspergillosis 216
  bumblefoot 213
  choosing 82, 85
  free flight training 143
  gauntlets 31, 163
  historically 8
  hunting training 156, 158–9, 161–4
  imprinting 82
  perches 23
enter, definition 221
environmental factors
  and aspergillosis 216
  and bumblefoot 213–14
  and choice of bird 85
Eurasian eagle owl (*Bubo bubo*) 60, 62–5, 76,
  78–9, 168, 204
  training 175–8, 180–3
eyass 68, 221
eyrie 221

falconer's knot 71, 86, 87–8, 89, 92, 99–103
falcons (general) 20, 24, 31, 75, 122
  aspergillosis 216
  bumblefoot 210
  free flight training 141
  historically 12–16
  hoods 108, 114–17
  hunting training 156
  lure training 32, 126–37
  perches 23
  see also individual species of falcon
feaking 218, 221
feathers
  donor feathers (imping) 35, 221
  hard penned 221
  moulting 71, 74, 75, 205, 221
  nutritional supplements 205
  rousing 221
feeding/food 202–7
  diet 202, 205, 220
  food pouch/pot 29, 31, 32
  food preparation 206–7
  and free flight training 141, 143, 149, 154–5
  on the glove 72–3, 86, 89, 91, 92–5, 106–7,
  184, 202–3, 204–5
  and hunting training 156–67
  and lure training 126–37

natural beak wearing 218
and owl training 168–87
owlets 178
owls 184–7
  and recall training 119, 121, 122, 124–5
roadkill 205
wild food 205
feet
  moisturising 39
  see also bumblefoot; talons
  ferruginous buzzard, hunting training
  159
flushing 44, 49, 108, 143, 144, 156, 221
flying jesses 24, 26, 28, 29, 180
  attaching 118, 168–9
  free flight training 145–8
  owls 168–9, 180, 181–2
flying weight 68, 71, 91, 118, 122, 144
  owls 60, 71, 182, 184, 186–7
food pouch/pot 29, 31, 32
free flight aviary 194–5
free flight training 138–55
  owls 181–7
free-lofted birds 75–6, 182
furniture 20

gauntlet 31–2
  eagle 162–3
  feeding on 72–3, 86, 89, 91, 92–5, 106–7,
  184, 202–3, 204–5
  hunting training 160, 162–3
  hygiene 202–3
  tying bird to 100–3
golden eagle (*Aquila chrysaetos*) 56–9, 83, 85,
  218
  aspergillosis 216
  beaks 218
  hunting training 156, 159, 161
goshawk (*Accipiter gentilis*) 44, 48, 49, 50–1, 52
  aspergillosis 216
  free flight training 143–4
  hunting training 156, 159
gyrfalcon (*Falco rusticolus*) 12, 16, 53, 210,
  216, 217

hacking 221
haggard 68
hand-rearing 82, 85, 168, 187, 221
handling the bird 86–105
hard penned 221
Harris's hawk (*Parabuteo unicinctus*) 44–7, 49,
  86, 89, 90–1, 112–13, 204
  hunting training 156, 159, 161, 166–7
  perch 22–3
  talon clipping and coping 38–9
hole punch tool 30
hood 24, 30
  fitting 108–17
  and free flight training 138, 141, 143–4
  and hunting training 161
  and lure training 126–7, 129, 134–5
hunting training 156–67

INDEX/PICTURE CREDITS

imping 35, 221
imprint raptors 82, 85, 168, 187, 221
injuries 213, 220
intermewed 221

jesses *see* flying jesses; mews jesses

knots 71, 86, 87–8, 89, 99–103

leash 26, 28, 28–9, 30, 71, 75, 86, 86, 184–6
  falconer's knot 86–9
  free flight training 140–1, 150–4
  initial training 96–103
  owls 184–6
  tying 150–4
licencing 35
lure 32, 119, 122, 221
  free flight training 141
  lure training 126–37

manning 84, 91, 221
mantling 95, 221
mews jesses 28
  attaching to swivel 181–3
  owls 179, 180–3
moulting 71, 74, 75, 205, 221
mutes 192, 221

owls (general) 16
  anklets 181
  aspergillosis 216
  attaching the creance 172–4, 186
  choice of 83
  feeding 178, 184–7
  flying free 175–8
  flying jesses 29, 168–9, 181
  flying weight 182, 184, 186–7
  free flight training 181–7
  initial training 170–1, 178

leash 184–6
mews jesses 179
mood swings 171
physiology 171, 175, 178
safety position 71, 180
swivel 181–3
telemetry tracker 186–7
training 168–87
ownership, laws of 12

parent-reared birds 78–9, 82, 85, 91, 168, 187
passing 141, 221
pellet 221
perches 20–4, 220
picking up the bird 99–103
pitch 221
pododermatitis (bumblefoot) *see* bumblefoot
pouch/pot 29, 31, 32
preen 221

quail (as food) 202
quarry 16, 35, 221
  of different species 44, 49, 55, 60
  hunting training 156–67

rats (as food) 202, 205
recall training 118–25
rearing 82
  imprint raptors 82, 85, 168, 187, 221
  parent-reared birds 78–9, 82, 85, 91, 168, 187
red-tailed hawk (*buteo jamaicensis*) 42–44, 212, 216
  hunting training 156, 159

safety position 24, 71, 71, 75, 86, 90, 122–3, 180
saker falcon (*Falco Cherrug*) 55, 56

slip 156, 221
snowy owl (*Bubo scandiacus*) 216
soaring 44, 143, 221
Steppe eagle (*Aquila nipalensis*) 82, 158, 160–4
stooping 44, 52, 156, 221
swivel 26, 28–9, 120–2, 144–5, 221
  attaching to mews jesses 181–3
  and the leash 184–6
swooping 55, 161, 164

talons 218
  cutting 34, 35, 36–9, 218
taming 98
telemetry tracker 31, 33, 138–55, 186–7
tethering 75–7, 86, 181
tiercel 221
tracker 31, 33, 138–55, 186–7
training
  free flight training 138–55
  hunting training 156–67
  lure training 126–37
  owls 168–87
  recall training 118–25
  training aviary 198–9
travel box 33, 140, 178

Ural owl 72–3

veterinary care 35, 220

weighing scales 20–1, 91, 104–5
weight/weighing
  flying weight 68, 71, 91, 118, 122, 144
  flying weight of owls 60, 71, 182, 184, 186–7
  and moulting 75
  scales 20–1, 91, 104–5
  weighing the bird 104–5, 106, 118, 119

yarak 221

PICTURE CREDITS

Alamy: 8 (Ahmad Karimi), 9 (Damian Byrne), 10 top (Granger Historical Picture Archive), 12/13 (Album), 17 (Roger Coulam), 18/20 (Ann and Steve Toon), 23 (Jill Morgan), 24 top (Juniors Bildarchiv GmbH), 24 bottom (Lee Beel), 29 (Peter Szekely), 31 right (Richard Mittleman Gon2Foto), 32 bottom (Barry Mason), 74 (Nature Picture Library), 75 (Lee Beel), 188/189 (Jaap Bleijenberg), 192 (Bari Paramarta), 194/195 (chris24), 210/211 & 213 (Associated Press), 214 (Manuel Goerlich Senis)

Coda Falconry/Elliot Manarin: 21/22, 25/26, 28, 30 top & bottom, 31 left, 32 top left, 32 top right, 33/34, 36/39, 70/71, 80/81, 83 top, 84/85, 86–187, 198–207, 215, 219

Dreamstime: 6/7 (Longtaildog), 16 (Profmym), 27 (Ian Dyball), 40/41 (Mycteria), 42 (Ondrejprosicky), 44 (Ca2hill), 45 (Jaypierstorff), 46/47 (Ondrejprosicky), 48 (Salonmriya), 50/51 (Mycteria), 52/53 (Katiekk), 54 (Rinus Baak), 55 (Kertuee), 56/57 (Vladsokolovsky), 58/59 (Geoffrey Kuchera), 61 (6bears), 62/63 (Whitcomberd), 64/65 (Ondrejprosicky), 68 (6bears), 69 (Chris2766), 72/73 (Sduben), 76 (Sduben), 82 (Ondrejprosicky), 83 bottom (Sduben), 85 (Milkovasa), 190/191 (Samumvcc), 193 (Linda Bestwick), 212 (Dndavis), 217 (Sduben)

Getty Images: 14/15 (Jaromir)

Public Domain: 10 bottom (Raghvendra99674010), 11 (Aavindraa)

Shutterstock: 5 (Vishnevskiy Vasily), 30 middle (Mark Humphreys), 66/67 (Milan Rybar), 77 (Bob L Parker), 78/79 (Albert Beukhof), 197 (Content Melnikoff), 208/209 (Jim Cumming), 218 (Ian Duffield)